Drupal 8 Configuration Management

Make the most of Drupal 8's coolest new feature—the Configuration Management system

Stefan Borchert

Anja Schirwinski

BIRMINGHAM - MUMBAI

Drupal 8 Configuration Management

First published: March 2015

Production reference: 1130315

Published by Packt Publishing Ltd.
Livery Place
35 Livery Street
Birmingham B3 2PB, UK.

ISBN 978-1-78398-520-3

www.packtpub.com

Credits

Authors
Stefan Borchert
Anja Schirwinski

Reviewers
Greg Dunlap
Johannes Haseitl
Thomas Keitel
Jose A. Reyero
Dev Saran

Commissioning Editor
Julian Ursell

Acquisition Editor
Kevin Colaco

Content Development Editor
Shubhangi Dhamgaye

Technical Editor
Indrajit A. Das

Copy Editors
Alfida Paiva
Adithi Shetty

Project Coordinator
Harshal Ved

Proofreaders
Stephen Copestake
Maria Gould

Indexer
Priya Sane

Production Coordinator
Alwin Roy

Cover Work
Alwin Roy

About the Authors

Stefan Borchert has been working with Drupal for more than 9 years. In the community, he is better known by his nickname stBorchert. He contributes to Drupal by writing contributed modules, helping with Drupal Core, and providing help to new contributors as a project application review administrator. He is a founding partner and senior Drupal developer at undpaul, a Drupal Digital Agency based in Germany.

Anja Schirwinski got to know Drupal more than 8 years ago as a themer/site builder and went on to build several very different web applications with it for the company she worked for. She has been a participating member of the Drupal community since 2007, known by the nickname aschiwi.

From 2009-2010, Anja was the deputy chair of the Drupal Initiative, a registered association that promotes Drupal in Germany. She is the cofounder and CEO of undpaul, one of the first Drupal-only digital agencies in Germany. She founded the company in 2010 with friends she met at a local Drupal user group.

About the Reviewer

Thomas Keitel, also known as hctom on the Web, started with computers as a kid using an Amiga 500 for his first graphic designs. When technology evolved, he became more and more interested in learning how to program and design for the Web. He completed his training as a digital media designer in 2003, focusing on a combination of development and design. Being more of a self-learner, he taught himself several web programming languages before finally settling for PHP. This got him started with Drupal in 2007. Over the years, he built a wide range of Drupal sites from small corporate sites to big community and content portals.

In August 2014, he started working for undpaul, one of Germany's oldest Drupal-only digital agencies.

www.PacktPub.com

Support files, eBooks, discount offers, and more

For support files and downloads related to your book, please visit www.PacktPub.com.

Did you know that Packt offers eBook versions of every book published, with PDF and ePub files available? You can upgrade to the eBook version at www.PacktPub.com and as a print book customer, you are entitled to a discount on the eBook copy. Get in touch with us at service@packtpub.com for more details.

At www.PacktPub.com, you can also read a collection of free technical articles, sign up for a range of free newsletters and receive exclusive discounts and offers on Packt books and eBooks.

https://www2.packtpub.com/books/subscription/packtlib

Do you need instant solutions to your IT questions? PacktLib is Packt's online digital book library. Here, you can search, access, and read Packt's entire library of books.

Why subscribe?

- Fully searchable across every book published by Packt
- Copy and paste, print, and bookmark content
- On demand and accessible via a web browser

Free access for Packt account holders

If you have an account with Packt at www.PacktPub.com, you can use this to access PacktLib today and view 9 entirely free books. Simply use your login credentials for immediate access.

Table of Contents

Preface

In professional web development, especially when working in teams of any size, configuration management is one of the most important tasks when it comes to keeping track of configuration changes.

The Wikipedia article for Software Configuration Management states that "In software engineering, software configuration management (SCM) is the task of tracking and controlling changes in the software, which is part of the larger cross-discipline field of configuration management. SCM practices include revision control and the establishment of baselines. If something goes wrong, SCM can determine what was changed and who changed it. If a configuration is working well, SCM can determine how to replicate it across many hosts."

So what is configuration in Drupal terms?

In Drupal, configuration includes topics such as content types, fields, menus, or text formats. Creating or changing a configuration on a live site poses a high risk and makes changes untraceable. Questions such as who made a change, and when and why it was made, cannot be answered.

Up until Drupal 7, Drupal had all configuration stored in the database. By Drupal 7, most professional Drupal developers kept track of their configuration changes by exporting them to code, the most popular option being the Features module, and version-controlling it with a version control system such as Git.

How it works in Drupal 8

When planning for Drupal 8, the so-called Configuration Management Initiative was led by Greg Dunlap in order to make developers' lives easier. Configuration still lives in the database, but can be easily exported to YAML text files. You can now deploy a configuration from one environment to another (between cloned instances of the same site). This capability replaces the need for various contributed modules such as Features, Strongarm, and Context.

This book will teach you everything you need to know about Drupal 8's brand new configuration system. We hope you enjoy it.

What this book covers

Chapter 1, Understanding Configuration Management, will give you a quick overview of Drupal 8's hottest new feature: Configuration Management. You will learn what types of configuration exist, why managing configuration is a good idea, and how to get started with it. We will introduce you to version control and show you some best practices. We will provide a look at the several ways in which configuration was managed in Drupal 7 and then show how Drupal 8 approaches the problem.

Chapter 2, Configuration Management for Administrators, provides an introduction on how to use Configuration Management for users who are not developers, but administrators of a Drupal website who want to make use of the advantages of this new feature. We will show you how to use the Configuration Management interface and how to create a copy of your website, and you will learn how to move a configuration made on one site to another site.

Chapter 3, Drupal 8's Take on Configuration Management, will show you the inner workings of the Configuration Management system in Drupal 8. You will learn about config and schema files, and read about the difference between simple configuration and configuration entities.

Chapter 4, The Configuration Management API, will teach you how to get your hands dirty and learn about the Configuration Management API of Drupal 8. Here, you will dive into the Simple Configuration API and learn how configuration can be overridden. Later, you will take a closer look at how to create custom configuration entity types, and we'll also teach you about the configuration's context system.

Chapter 5, The Anatomy of Schema Files, covers schema files and explains how Drupal uses them for Configuration Management. You will learn about the structure of schema files used by Drupal and write your own schema for custom configuration.

Chapter 6, Adding Configuration Management to Your Module, will teach you how to access configuration objects and how schema files are structured in the previous chapters. (You will surely want to know how to get all this fancy stuff into your shiny new module for Drupal 8). You will learn how to include the default configuration in custom modules, how to define and use your own configuration, and how to create configuration forms.

Chapter 7, Upgrading Your Drupal 7 Variables to the Drupal 8 Configuration, will show you ways to convert your Drupal 7 variables into Drupal 8 Configuration objects and how to provide an upgrade path in your modules.

Chapter 8, Managing Configuration for Multilingual Websites, allows you to build comprehensive multilingual websites in which you can display a site's content in different languages and translate the user interface. While many features were built into Drupal's core in previous versions, building multilingual sites remained a very painful task. In this chapter, we will take a look at how Drupal 7 deals with different languages on a site and how Drupal 8 is trying to fix weaknesses from previous versions.

Chapter 9, Useful Tools and Getting Help, provides a list of links and tools provided by the Drupal community; these will be useful if you reach a point where you need help when dealing with Configuration Management.

What you need for this book

To follow along with this book, you need an installation of Drupal 8, preferably in a local development environment. There's some good documentation about setting up a local development environment at `https://www.drupal.org/setting-up-development-environment`. Specific system requirements for all Drupal versions are listed at `https://www.drupal.org/requirements`.

To follow the code examples, you will need a text editor or an IDE. There's a good list of suitable software at `https://www.drupal.org/node/147789`.

Who this book is for

Drupal Configuration Management is intended for anyone who uses Drupal 8 to build websites, whether they are a hobbyist using Drupal for the first time, or a long-time Drupal site builder, or a professional web developer.

Conventions

In this book, you will find a number of styles of text that distinguish between different kinds of information. Here are some examples of these styles, and an explanation of their meaning.

Code words in text, database table names, folder names, filenames, file extensions, pathnames, dummy URLs, user input, and Twitter handles are shown as follows: "Finally, to run the migrations, we need to execute the Drush command `migrate-manifest`."

A block of code is set as follows:

```
# Example for Drupal 7 to Drupal 8 migration
d7_cm_example_settings
d7_cm_example_block
d7_block
d7_filter_format
```

New terms and **important words** are shown in bold. Words that you see on the screen, in menus or dialog boxes for example, appear in the text like this: "On this page, you simply select **Simple configuration** as the configuration type, paste the copied configuration value into the text area, and click on **Import**."

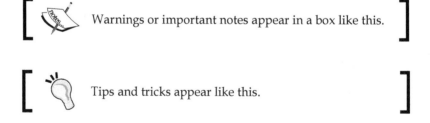

Warnings or important notes appear in a box like this.

Tips and tricks appear like this.

Reader feedback

Feedback from our readers is always welcome. Let us know what you think about this book—what you liked or may have disliked. Reader feedback is important for us to develop titles that you really get the most out of.

To send us general feedback, simply send an e-mail to feedback@packtpub.com, and mention the book title via the subject of your message.

If there is a topic that you have expertise in and you are interested in either writing or contributing to a book, see our author guide on www.packtpub.com/authors.

Customer support

Now that you are the proud owner of a Packt book, we have a number of things to help you to get the most from your purchase. You can contact the authors at http://drupal-8-configuration-management.undpaul.com if you are facing a problem with any aspect of this book, and they will do their best to address it.

Downloading the example code

You can download the example code files for all Packt books you have purchased from your account at http://www.packtpub.com. If you purchased this book elsewhere, you can visit http://www.packtpub.com/support and register to have the files e-mailed directly to you.

Errata

Although we have taken every care to ensure the accuracy of our content, mistakes do happen. If you find a mistake in one of our books—maybe a mistake in the text or the code—we would be grateful if you would report this to us. By doing so, you can save other readers from frustration and help us improve subsequent versions of this book. If you find any errata, please report them by visiting http://www.packtpub.com/submit-errata, selecting your book, clicking on the **errata submission form** link, and entering the details of your errata. Once your errata are verified, your submission will be accepted and the errata will be uploaded on our website, or added to any list of existing errata, under the Errata section of that title. Any existing errata can be viewed by selecting your title from http://www.packtpub.com/support.

Piracy

Piracy of copyright material on the Internet is an ongoing problem across all media. At Packt, we take the protection of our copyright and licenses very seriously. If you come across any illegal copies of our works, in any form, on the Internet, please provide us with the location address or website name immediately so that we can pursue a remedy.

Please contact us at `copyright@packtpub.com` with a link to the suspected pirated material.

We appreciate your help in protecting our authors, and our ability to bring you valuable content.

Questions

You can contact us at `questions@packtpub.com` if you are having a problem with any aspect of the book, and we will do our best to address it.

1
Understanding Configuration Management

In this first chapter, we will give you a quick overview of Drupal 8's hottest new feature: **Configuration Management**. You will learn what types of configuration exist, why managing configuration is a good idea, and how to get started with it. We will introduce you to version control and show some best practices. We will also provide a look at the several ways in which configuration was managed in Drupal 7, and then show how Drupal 8 approaches the problem.

An introduction to Configuration Management

The general definition of the term "Configuration Management" is somewhat different from the definition of Configuration Management in Drupal 8. To make things easier, we will focus on explaining what Configuration Management is in Drupal terms.

Configuration Management in Drupal 8 aims at making configuration manageable across different environments by allowing us to store configuration in files instead of the database.

Let's start by defining what configuration is, and what other types of information exist in Drupal 8.

Configuration

Configuration is the information about your site that is not content and is meant to be more permanent, such as the name of your site, the content types, fields, and views you have defined.

Content

Content is the information meant to be displayed on your site, such as articles, basic pages, images, files, and so on.

Session

This is the information about an individual user's interactions with the site, such as whether they are logged in.

State

This is information of a temporary nature about the current state of your site. Examples include the time when Cron was last run, whether node access permissions need rebuilding, and so on.

Why manage configuration?

It's simple to explain why configuration that is only saved in the database is bad. You can't keep track of any changes (who made what change, and when); it's hard to work with a group of people (you simply can't get their changes without using their SQL dump, and using their dump would delete your work); and, if you build something on a development environment, how do you get it to the live site? You get the gist. We want our configuration in files, and Drupal 8 gives us just that.

Before Drupal 8, a variety of methods were used to transport configuration from one environment to another — for example, from a development environment to a production environment.

These included some rather bad methods such as writing down the process to manually recreate the same configuration, which is error-prone; dumping the development database in the live site, which loses all content created in the meantime; and some better but rather time-consuming methods, such as writing update hooks or using the contributed module Features to export configuration to a module. The latter is one of the most used methods in Drupal 7 because it works well most of the time, produces well-arranged files, and can be used without having to write any code, which is good because anyone can create a Feature without having to know how to code.

Even though you can use the new Configuration Management system without a version control system such as Git, it's at its best when used with one. Version-controlling your configuration allows you to track document changes. Later in this chapter, we will show you how to get the best out of version-controlling your configuration. Version-controlled Configuration Management is crucial to developing and maintaining quality in a Drupal project, especially when working with a team of developers. Exposing all developers to the same code and providing a history for the code increases efficiency a lot.

At first, it might seem frustrating to have to learn something new. However, software tends to change over time, and changes are hard to track using just your memory. This is really one of the best ways to improve your project and save your time and money, so make sure you learn it!

Tracking configuration changes

Drupal 8's new Configuration Management system can be used without a version control system, but if you want to really improve your process, you should use it in combination with version control. Having organized and versioned code helps prevent mistakes and duplicated efforts between multiple developers; it serves as documentation of the project's history and can show who worked on what and, very importantly, why.

There are others, but we are going to talk about Git as our example version control tool because it's used by the Drupal community and offers everything we need in terms of functionality, scalability, and ease-of-use.

 Use a version control tool such as Git to get the best out of the Configuration Management system!

The best time to start with versioned Configuration Management is at the beginning of the development. However, it's never too late, even if your project has been started or even finished for a while. Check your Drupal site configuration, organize it, and put everything in a Git repository. Now, you have a good starting point from which to manage and document any changes that will be made to the project in the future.

Some version control best practices

So let's see what will really improve the development process when using version control.

Using a project management tool

You will achieve the best results if you put your work tasks in a project management tool such as the free and open source tool Redmine. If you're not used to working with a project management tool, it might take some discipline to keep track of your work this way, but it has so many advantages. The ticket holds information about what needs to be done and you can use the ticket's comments to discuss requirements, give status updates, or report problems.

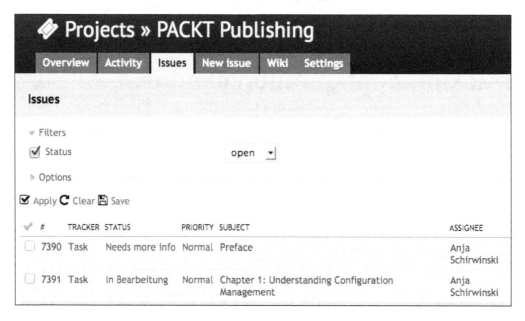

Most project management tools also have some sort of ID for each ticket. You can use the ticket ID in your Git commit messages, which is a very good way to know why a commit was made.

Meaningful commit messages

Commit messages are a very important part of your code documentation when working with version control. When looking for something that was done in the past, you will first scan through the commit messages, as shown in the following screenshot:

yesterday at 15:51	Issue #7466: Changed map type to google-roadmap
yesterday at 15:51	Issue #7444: Enable Field Templates for view modes
yesterday at 15:51	Issue #7444: Added deletion of field_location_route_planner to update script
yesterday at 15:51	Issue #7444: Remove field_location_route_planner
yesterday at 15:51	Issue #7466: Disabled tooltip, changed label of popup field to be more logic
yesterday at 15:51	Issue #7466: Only show locations with a company group selected
yesterday at 15:51	Issue #7444: Fixed labels and descriptions of location, removed title location in map view
yesterday at 15:51	Issue #7466: Fixed wrong variable name

It makes no sense at all to just use a commit message such as *stuff* or even *asdf*. You might laugh, but we've seen both of these in real-world projects. When you start out with version control, it will take some discipline to write meaningful commit messages, but it's really worth it when you come across a bug and are looking for code that might have caused it. Make sure you always use the ticket ID that your project management tool provides and put it at the beginning of your commit message. When you find the commit that causes the problem, the ID will give you more information about what was done there and for what reason.

 Small and well-structured commits are more effective.

Also, make commits small! Do not wait until your workday is over to commit everything you did on that day. This will make it more difficult to go through the changes in that specific commit. For example, make each new contributed module you add to your project a separate commit; do not add 5 modules at once or a module together with other code or configuration.

Meaningful branches

Tickets that require a lot of work should be worked on in a separate branch. When you name that branch, make sure you use your ticket ID at the beginning – for instance, `1234-publications`, as shown in the following screenshot:

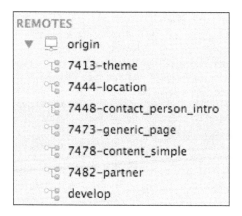

A look back at Drupal 7

Configuration Management in Drupal 7 isn't as simple as its equivalent in Drupal 8. In Drupal 7, almost the entire configuration set on a site is stored in the database by default. This includes simple variables, content types and field configuration, settings from custom or contributed modules, and so on.

Using the database to store settings makes it really hard to track configuration changes or roll back a bunch of settings to a state defined earlier.

Unfortunately, there is no real standard for Configuration Management in Drupal 7, but there are several ways to manage site and module settings in the code.

We will take a short look at the following five different approaches:

- Manual Configuration Management
- The `hook_install()` / `hook_update_N()` function
- The Features module
- The Configuration Management module
- Storing configuration variables in `settings.php`

Manual Configuration Management

Many users of Drupal manage their configuration manually. They try to remember each setting they've made in the local development environment and then recreate every step on the live site. At first sight, this seems to be very fast and easy, but if you have to manually set permissions for some roles multiple times, you'll never want to do this manually again after hearing there are much better ways.

Additionally, you will never know if a setting has changed and all of your configuration will not be version-controlled (because it only exists in the database). Also, it makes working in a team much more painful than necessary.

If you ever want to share configuration between two or more instances of a site, don't do this.

[Don't use manual Configuration Management!]

The hook_install()/hook_update_N() function

Install and update hooks are the simplest way to manage configuration on a Drupal 7 site in code. The basic idea behind this approach is to set configuration values while installing a module or running `update.php`. Within the `.install` file of a custom module, you implement `hook_install()` and/or `hook_update_N()`, and add the code needed to set the configuration to these functions:

```php
<?php

/**
 * Implements hook_install().
 */
function my_module_install() {
  // Set site name.
  variable_set('site_name', 'Configuration Management');
}
```

In this example, we simply set the variable `site_name` to the `Configuration Management` value, so the name of our site will be updated to this value after enabling the module. The possibilities given here are nearly endless. In addition to setting simple variables, you might add new roles, update block settings, or even create new content types. However, while it's technically possible, it is not recommended and not very simple to export complex configuration (think of fields or views). Also, you need a developer to actually write the code.

Unfortunately, this is *one-way configuration management*, so there is no way to automatically save changes that you have made on the site's configuration back to code. You have to update the code manually with the new settings (for example, add a new implementation of `hook_update_N()`).

Additionally, you do not have any chance to see which settings were changed by a user. If you want to save the current state of configuration, you need to go through all settings set in `hook_install()` or `hook_update_N()` and compare them with the current settings on the site.

The Features module

To manage configuration in Drupal 7, most people use the Features module (`https://drupal.org/project/features`). If you need a simple tool to export your configuration and put it under version control, Features is the module to work with in Drupal 7.

What is the Features module?

To quote James Sansbury from Lullabot:

> *"The Features module is a module that creates other modules called features."*

In other words, Features helps you to put your site's configuration into code so that you can keep track of changes and simply share it with other sites. It was originally created to serve another purpose: to group multiple configurations for one use-case so you could package actual site features and use them in different sites. However, due to a lack of alternatives, it ended up becoming popular as a tool to manage Drupal configuration.

Features works by using so-called components that hold information about configuration objects provided by Drupal itself or contributed modules.

Features uses different types of components: configuration objects that live in code without the need for an instance in the database (exportable components) and so-called faux-exportable components that must exist in the database. Exports of faux-exportable components are used to synchronize configuration objects in the database, so the settings are always up-to-date.

To make an object exportable, you can write a module and use your own default hook handling and export generation. The default hook provides a default state of your configuration object that is directly used on the site or synchronized with the database (depending on the needs of this object).

A very simple example of an object exported using a default hook is a content type. Custom modules can provide their own content types using `hook_node_info()`:

```php
<?php

/**
 * Implements hook_node_info().
 */
function cm_blog_node_info() {
  return array(
    'blog' => array(
      'name' => t('Blog'),
      'base' => 'blog',
      'description' =>t('Use for multi-user blogs.'),
    ),
  );
}
?>
```

This simple example (taken from `api.drupal.org`) defines a new content type with the machine name *blog*. Additionally, it sets the human-readable name to *Blog* and adds a short description to the type, so users know about its purpose.

A better way to make custom configuration objects exportable is to integrate the module with the `CTools Export` API.

> The `CTools Export` API has been designed to provide a standardized way to export and import objects in Drupal. Developers simply add some special keys to the object's schema and implement a load function as well as a save function.

Using the `CTools Export` API, Features will automatically integrate with your module and handle the export and synchronization of your components. Prominent representatives of contributed modules that implement this in Drupal 7 are Views and Panels.

Creating a Feature

Creating a Feature is very easy. Using the user interface of the Features module, you simply add the components you would like to export to the newly created module. While generating the new module, Features uses the defined default hooks or the `CTools Export` API to save the information about the components to code so you don't need to write the code yourself. While writing the code may be fairly easy for content types (as shown previously), writing down the complete configuration of a field, an image style, or even a view is not so simple, and you do not want to do this manually. With Features, you only need a few clicks to get the configuration into code. Take a look at the following screenshot:

In the preceding example, we selected the content type **Blog** along with some permissions. As you can see, Features automatically added the required dependencies to other modules along with the information about the fields of the content type and common variables related to the type.

After adding everything you want to include in the export, you can download the feature or let Features directly create the files on your disk.

 If you create a new Feature, make sure you use a unique machine-readable name that does not conflict with any existing module. The best practice is to prepend the machine name with an abbreviation of your project or site name (in our example, cm_blog).

After downloading the Feature and enabling it in the same way as any other module, you are able to track changes to components in the Feature. For example, if you change the label of a field included in the Feature, the Feature will be shown as overridden. With the help of the Diff module, it even displays each modified component as follows:

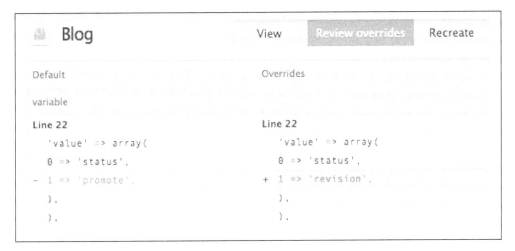

You can then choose between reverting the Feature to its default state (that's what you have in the code of your Feature), which would undo the change you made to your field label, or you can update the Feature, which gives you the modified values in code, so you can share it with others or distribute it to another environment.

Both tasks can either be done using the Feature UI or Drush, which is much faster.

The settings to export with Features

Basically, all components that rely on the CTools Export API, or on modules that define default hooks, may be exported.

These include the following:

- **Variables**: These are exported using the Strongarm module, which implements the `CTools Export` API for all entries in the `variables` table of Drupal
- **Views**: These are exported using the default hook: `hook_views_default_views()`
- **Content types**: These are directly exported by the Features API using Drupal's `hook_node_info()`
- **Field definitions**: These are exported using default hooks defined by Features itself
- **And many more**: These include text formats, image styles, and rules (`http://www.drupal.org/project/rules`)

The settings to not export with Features

While some components may theoretically be exportable, it is not always sensible to do this. For example, exporting cache variables or variables that store timestamps such as `cron_last`, which stores the date when the last cron was run, would result in constantly overridden Features. There is also no benefit in having components such as this in code, because you can't actively change it, and you don't need to know its value for anything.

As a general rule of thumb, you should never export components that change often, such as timestamps or status variables.

The Configuration Management module

The Configuration Management module is the latest approach we will take a look at here. While Features was never really intended to do real Configuration Management, the Configuration Management module takes some core concepts from the Drupal 8 Configuration Management Initiative and makes them available for Drupal 7.

The main concept behind this module is the data storage architecture. It defines an activestore and a datastore to manage the configuration of a site. The activestore represents the current state of an individual configuration component (for example, a variable in the database) whereas the datastore is defined as the file that contains the default state of the component.

After changing the value of a component tracked by the Configuration Management module, you can save its value back to the datastore (the module updates the corresponding files for you) so that you can track the changes in your version control system.

Looking at the export of this configuration in the following screenshot, you will notice many similarities. This is due to the fact that both modules use the CTools Export API and nearly the same default hooks to import/export the data.

```
$data = (object) array(                function cm_blog_node_info() {
  'type' => 'blog',                       $items = array(
  'name' => 'Blog',                         'blog' => array(
  'description' => '',                        'name' => t('Blog'),
  'has_title' => '1',                         'base' => 'node_content',
  'title_label' => 'Title',                   'description' => '',
  'base' => 'node_content',                   'has_title' => '1',
  'help' => '',                               'title_label' => t('Title'),
);                                            'help' => '',
                                            ),
                                          );
$dependencies = array();                  return $items;
                                        }
```

The main advantage of the Configuration Management module in comparison to Features is the reduction to pure Configuration Management. There is no possibility for a developer to extend the export with custom code (that is `hook_form_alter()` or `hook_menu()`) as is done often when exporting configuration objects with Features. The export simply contains the components you want to put under version control and nothing more.

Storing configuration variables in settings.php

There is one more way to store settings back in Drupal 7: your site's settings.php, which you know from storing your database details in it. The Drupal installation process and Drupal modules use the `variables` table to store different types of information that will be used at runtime. The values of these variables can be overridden in the `settings.php` file. Every module, when enabled, may add variables that can be altered in the configuration setting. One example is the variable named `theme_default`, which sets the default theme.

Variables stored inside your `settings.php` file's `$conf` array will override whatever is in the variables table of your database. This is really useful when you need different configuration for different environments, such as local, staging, and production.

There is a complete list of default variables available on a fresh installation of Drupal at `https://www.drupal.org/node/1525472`.

How Drupal 8 takes care of Configuration Management

Drupal 8 totally changes the way configuration is managed on a site. The configuration can be stored in files instead of the database, so it is not a problem to put it under version control.

All default configuration defined and used by a module must be able to be stored in special configuration files using the YAML specification and the `.yml` file extension. YAML is short for YAML Ain't Markup Language; according to its creators, YAML is *a human-friendly data serialization standard for all programming languages*. In short, it's easier to read and write. Each module provides its own default configuration files in a special folder named `config`, which makes it easy to see which configuration a module provides. Taking the core system module as an example, you will find several files in the `config` directory responsible for all configurations that the system module handles on the site.

How to start using Configuration Management

By default, Drupal 8 stores configuration in the site's database. During installation of your Drupal site, Drupal adds a directory within `sites/default/files` called `config_HASH`, where HASH is a long random string of letters and numbers, as shown in the following screenshot:

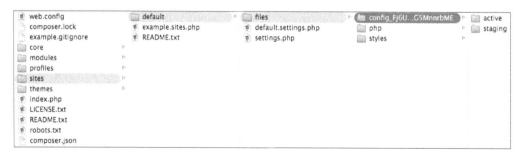

Using version control to keep track of configuration changes

Inside this `config` directory, there are two more directories: `active` and `staging`. Both contain no configuration files by default, but they each contain a helpful `README.txt`.

The contents of the `active` directory's `README.txt` are as follows:

If you change the configuration system to use file storage instead of the database for the active Drupal site configuration, this directory will contain the active configuration. By default, this directory will be empty. If you are using files to store the active configuration, and you want to move it between environments, files from this directory should be placed in the staging directory on the target server. To make this configuration active, visit `admin/config/development/configuration/sync` on the target server. For information about how to deploy configuration between servers, see `http://drupal.org/documentation/administer/config`.

The `staging` directory's `README.txt` explains the following points:

In order to start using Configuration Management to keep track of your configuration changes, all you have to do is export your current configuration and place it inside the `staging` directory as follows:

1. Go to `/admin/config/development/configuration/full/export` and use the **Export** button to download an archive of your site configuration, as shown in the following screenshot:

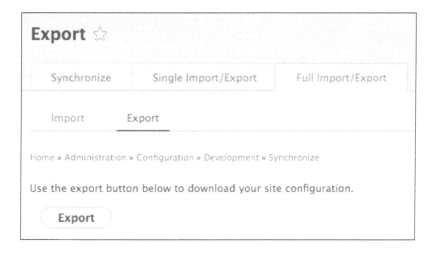

2. Save the archive inside the `sites/default/files/config_HASH/staging` folder of your Drupal source files and extract the contents of the archive. The result should look something like this:

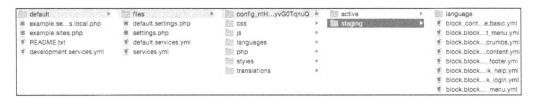

 If you're familiar with the Drupal command-line tool Drush, you can export configuration with a simple command. Check *Chapter 9, Useful Tools and Getting Help* for details.

You can find more detailed information in the next chapter, *Chapter 2, Configuration Management for Administrators*.

Types of configuration

There are two types of configuration in Drupal 8: simple configuration and configuration entities.

Simple configuration is basically the same as variables (that is, the site name or the number of nodes on the front page) and is used for single global settings.

Looking at the system module's configuration file `system.site.yml`, you see some examples for simple configuration. The file defines the default values for some of the main settings you will need on your site—that is, the site name or the default e-mail address:

```
name: 'Configuration Management in Drupal 8'
mail: 'info@example.com'
slogan: ''
page:
  403: ''
  404: ''
  front: user
langcode: en
```

As you can see, configuration can even be nested, so you can group settings.

Configuration entities are more complex than a simple configuration, and are used for objects that can have multiple copies such as content types or views.

Configuration storage and deploying between environments

Earlier in this chapter, we learned about the directory named `staging`. In this directory, you put the configuration you would like to import into a copy of your Drupal site—for example, to copy changes from your local environment to your production site. Simply export the new configuration from your local environment, place it in the staging directory of your production site (preferably by using version control), and import it later at `admin/config/development/configuration/sync`.

Note that, at the time of writing this book, the `active` directory is not used as originally intended. Its original purpose was to store the site's currently active configuration but, since that is now kept in the database, the `active` directory remains empty. This might change in future versions of Drupal 8.

Summary

Now you have a very complete overview of what Configuration Management is in Drupal 8 and why you should make use of it. You read about some best practices that show you how to best keep track of your changes with version control. You also learned about all the different ways to achieve some kind of Configuration Management in Drupal 7 and were given a basic introduction to the way it works in Drupal 8. Read on to find out how site administrators with no programming knowledge can use this system.

2
Configuration Management for Administrators

In the previous chapter, we learned about the general concept of Configuration Management and how we used Configuration Management in Drupal 7, or at least how we tried to do it.

This chapter will provide an introduction on how to use Configuration Management, for administrators (rather than developers) of a Drupal website who want to make use of the advantages of this new feature. We will show you how to use the Configuration Management interface, how to create a copy of your website, and how to move configuration made on one site to another site.

Why do we want to manage our configuration?

If you're not a developer, you might wonder what you need Configuration Management for. Up until now, you have probably made any changes right in the live website, which we call the *Production* website. For example, you might have added a field to a content type or moved a block to a new region. Sometimes, this works fine, sometimes it doesn't. When everything breaks, you may have to import a backup database, if you are lucky enough to have one. In the meantime, any visitors to your site may have seen a broken site and probably declined to come back. In professional web development, it's crucial to not make changes to the production website. Developers don't build new features in the live website but in a local copy of the site. Only when they are satisfied with the result will the changes go live.

We want to make our configuration live as fast as possible. We don't want to have to click our way through everything again. This is where Drupal 8's Configuration Management comes in. It allows you to easily export all configuration from a development copy of your site in a single `.zip` file and to import it to your live website.

> As a best practice, make sure you never make configuration changes in the production website or they will get lost the next time you import a configuration from your development site.

The development and production websites can be seen as follows:

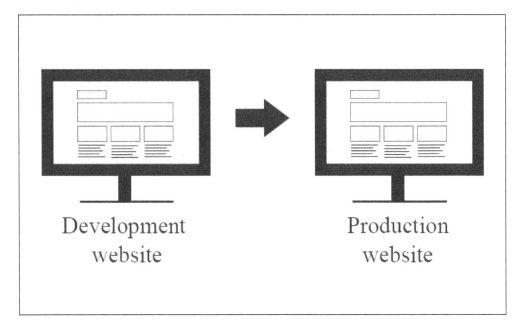

Making a clone of your site

For Configuration Management to work, you need to create an exact copy of your website. This might change in future versions of Drupal 8 but, at the time of writing, it has to be an exact copy. If you don't have a local development environment set up, that copy could be on the same server your website runs on. Copy the directory that Drupal runs in, and also copy the database. Make sure you change the database name in your `settings.php` file! It doesn't matter whether you use the original site or the copy as your development site or your production site. Just make the decision and then stick to it. Read on to find out how to export configuration from the development site and import it to the production site.

The Configuration Management interface

Let's take a look at Drupal 8's Configuration Management interface that was created for website administrators without programming knowledge. Now that you have two copies of your site, go to the one that you identify as your *Development Site*. As a simple example for the following explanations, we will use the configuration for *Site name*, which is the name you picked for your site during installation. Navigate to **Configuration | System | Site information**, change the contents of the site name, and save the page. You will find out how to apply those changes to what you identified as your Production Site.

You can find the Configuration Management interface by navigating to **Configuration | Configuration management** (`admin/config/development/configuration`), as shown in the following screenshot:

The interface options

In the first tab, **Synchronize**, you will see that there are no configuration changes, which means your site is using the configuration files from the database and that no changes were made to the site.

The second tab, **Single Import/Export**, allows you to import just a single configuration file. We will not go into details here but, if you're interested, you can read more about it in the Configuration Management documentation on Drupal.org at `https://drupal.org/documentation/administer/config`.

The third tab, **Full Import/Export**, is the option we will focus on now. After clicking on the tab, you will see two suboptions: **Import** and **Export**, as shown in the following screenshot:

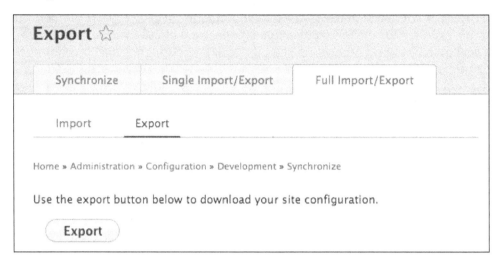

Go ahead and grab an export of your configuration. Clicking on the Export button will present you with the download of an archive file named `config.tar.gz`. Save this somewhere. Now, to actually do something with a configuration exported from your development site (let's call this **Site A** from here on), you need to go to the Production copy of your site (this will be **Site B** from here on). Refer to the *Making a clone of your site* section earlier in this chapter for how to do this.

Using full import/export

Now that you have exported your `config.tar.gz` file, we can get started with importing it into Site B.

Go to Site B and visit `admin/config/development/configuration/full/import` (Full Import/Export). Select your saved `config.tar.gz` from Site A and upload it, as shown in the following screenshot:

After uploading the file, go to the **Synchronize** page (`admin/config/development/ configuration`) and you should now see something like the following listing:

This page lists all the configuration changes, so you can check if everything is correct before completing the import.

In our example, there is a change to the file `system.site.yml`, because that is where the site name is stored. Drupal recognizes this, tells us that this file was changed, and allows you to view the differences, as shown in the following screenshot:

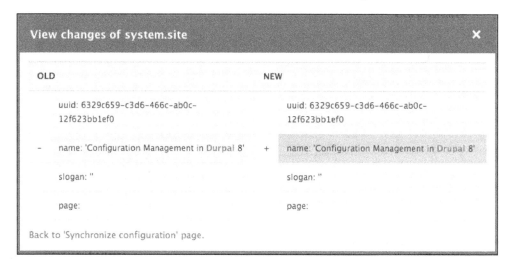

Once you're done checking the changes, close the popup and click on **Import all**.

The import may take up to a few minutes, depending on the number of differences between both sites, as shown in the following screenshot:

As soon as the import is finished, you will be redirected back to `admin/config/development/configuration`, where you can see that there are no further configuration changes, as shown in the following screenshot:

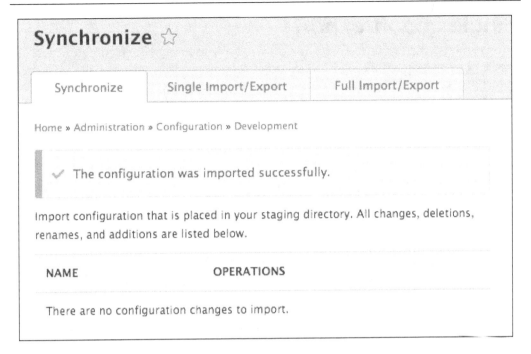

Now check your site information again at `admin/config/system/site-information`, and you will see that the site name from your **Site A** is now also in your **Site B**.

You will really enjoy this simple process once you're dealing with bigger changes to your site, such as a new or changed content type.

Although, theoretically, you should make all changes during development and export from there to production, sometimes direct changes to the production site may be necessary. To take those changes from the production site to development, simply export the full production site configuration, save the resulting config.tar.gz, and then import that into your development site. This will update the development site with your production changes. From here, you can continue making further changes on development and import back to production, as previously explained.

Single import/export

This is an advanced option. To use it, you will have to know which configuration type and name you're looking for. You don't need to use this option at all, but let's quickly cover what it's good for. You don't always need to synchronize the entire configuration between two installations. Sometimes, you only need to transfer a single configuration value or configuration entity from **Site A** to **Site B**.

Let's use our previous example and assume that you would like to copy the configuration for the site name to **Site B**. On **Site A**, change the site name again and then navigate to `admin/config/development/configuration/single/export`. You will need to select the type of configuration to export and (after selecting it) the specific name of the configuration. In our case, we select **Simple configuration** as the configuration type, and `system.site` as the name.

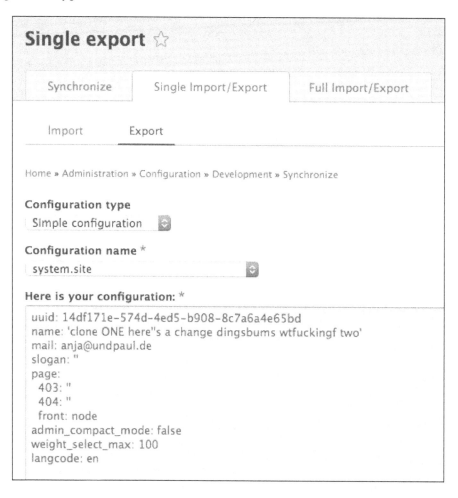

As soon as you select the configuration name, the contents of the text area will be updated with the current value of the selected configuration object.

Copy the contents of the text area and navigate to `admin/config/development/configuration/single/import` on **Site B**. On this page, you simply select **Simple configuration** as the configuration type, paste the copied configuration value into the text area, and click on **Import**. After confirming the action, you will be redirected back to the page when your configuration has been imported successfully.

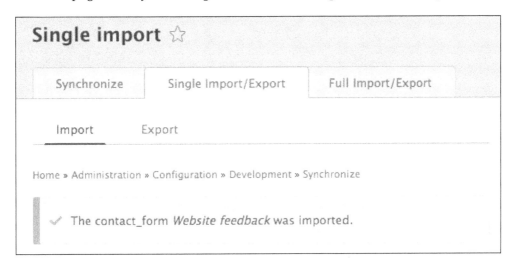

There is another way of moving your configuration from one site to another without using the interface. We will get to this in the next chapter.

Summary

In this chapter, we have learned how to use the Configuration Management interface and how to create a copy of our website, and also learned how to move a configuration made on one site to another site. In the next chapter, we will learn the inner workings of the Configuration Management system in Drupal 8.

3
Drupal 8's Take on Configuration Management

In this chapter, we will show you the inner workings of the Configuration Management system in Drupal 8. You will learn about config and schema files and read about the difference between simple configuration and configuration entities.

The config directory

During installation, Drupal adds a directory within `sites/default/files` called `config_HASH`, where HASH is a long random string of letters and numbers, as shown in the following screenshot:

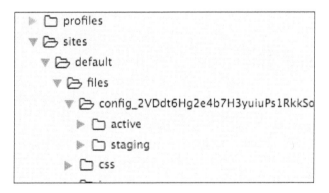

This sequence is a random hash generated during the installation of your Drupal site. It is used to add some protection to your configuration files. Additionally to the default restriction enforced by the `.htaccess` file within the subdirectories of the `config` directory that prevents unauthorized users from seeing the content of the directories. As a result, would be really hard for someone to guess the folder's name.

Within the `config` directory, you will see two additional directories that are empty by default (leaving the `.htaccess` and `README.txt` files aside).

One of the directories is called `active`. If you change the configuration system to use file storage instead of the database for active Drupal site configuration, this directory will contain the active configuration. If you did not customize the storage mechanism of the active configuration (we will learn later how to do this), Drupal 8 uses the database to store the active configuration.

The other directory is called `staging`. This directory is empty by default, but can host the configuration you want to be imported into your Drupal site from another installation. You will learn how to use this later on in this chapter.

A simple configuration example

First, we want to become familiar with configuration itself. If you look into the database of your Drupal installation and open up the `config` table , you will find the entire active configuration of your site, as shown in the following screenshot:

system.performance	a:6:{s:5:"cache";a:1:{s:4:"page";a:2:{s:12:"use internal";b:0;s:7:"max_age";i:0...
system.rss	a:3:{s:7:"channel";a:1:{s:11:"description";s:0:"";}s:5:"items";a:2:{s:5:"limit";i:1...
system.site	a:8:{s:4:"uuid";s:36:"6329c659-c3d6-466c-ab0c-xxx";s:4:"name";s:13:"cm...
system.theme	a:2:{s:5:"admin";s:5:"seven";s:7:"default";s:6:"bartik";}
system.theme.global	a:3:{s:7:"favicon";a:4:{s:8:"mimetype";s:24:"image/vnd.microsoft.icon";s:4:"p...

Depending on your site's configuration, table names may be prefixed with a custom string, so you'll have to look for a table name that ends with `config`.

Don't worry about the strange-looking text in the `data` column; this is the serialized content of the corresponding configuration. It expands to single configuration values — that is, `system.site.name`, which holds the value of the name of your site.

Changing the site's name in the user interface on `admin/config/system/site-information` will immediately update the record in the database; thus, put simply the records in the table are the current state of your site's configuration, as shown in the following screenshot:

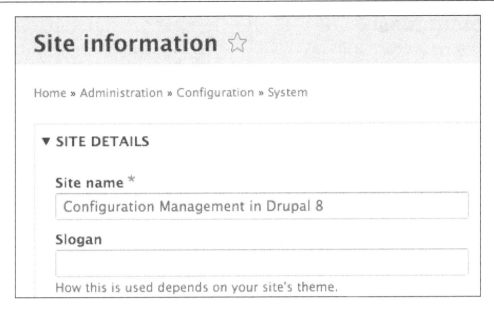

But where does the initial configuration of your site come from? Drupal itself and the modules you install must use some kind of default configuration that gets added to the active storage during installation.

Config and schema files – what are they and what are they used for?

In order to provide a default configuration during the installation process, Drupal (modules and profiles) comes with a bunch of files that hold the configuration needed to run your site. To make parsing of these files simple and enhance readability of these configuration files, the configuration is stored using the YAML format.

 YAML (http://yaml.org/) is a data-orientated serialization standard that aims for simplicity. With YAML, it is easy to map common data types such as lists, arrays, or scalar values.

Config files

Directly beneath the root directory of each module and profile defining or overriding configuration (either core or contrib), you will find a directory named `config`. Within this directory, there may be two more directories (although both are optional): `install` and `schema`.

Check the `image` module inside `core/modules` and take a look at its `config` directory, as shown in the following screenshot:

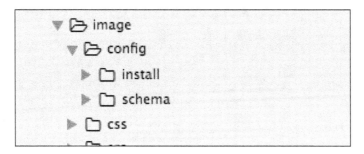

The `install` directory shown in the following screenshot contains all configuration values that the specific module defines or overrides and that are stored in files with the extension `.yml` (one of the default extensions for files in the YAML format):

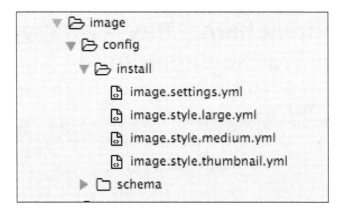

During installation, the values stored in these files are copied to the active configuration of your site. In the case of default configuration storage, the values are added to the `config` table; in file-based configuration storage mechanisms, on the other hand, the files are copied to the appropriate directories.

Looking at the filenames, you will see that they follow a simple convention: `<module name>.<type of configuration>[.<machine name of configuration object>].yml` (setting aside `<module name>.settings.yml` for now). The explanation is as follows:

- `<module name>`: This is the name of the module that defines the settings included in the file. For instance, the `image.style.large.yml` file contains settings defined by the image module.

- `<type of configuration>`: This can be seen as a type of group for configuration objects. The image module, for example, defines several image styles. These styles are a set of different configuration objects, so the group is defined as `style`. Hence, all configuration files that contain image styles defined by the image module itself are named `image.style.<something>.yml`.

 The same structure applies to blocks (`<block.block.*.yml>`), filter formats (`<filter.format.*.yml>`), menus (`<system.menu.*.yml>`), content types (`<node.type.*.yml>`), and so on.

- `<machine name of configuration object>`: The last part of the filename is the unique machine-readable name of the configuration object itself. In our examples from the image module, you see three different items: `large`, `medium`, and `thumbnail`. These are exactly the three image styles you will find on `admin/config/media/image-styles` after installing a fresh copy of Drupal 8. The image styles are shown in the following screenshot:

Schema files

The primary reason schema files were introduced into Drupal 8 is multilingual support. A tool was needed to identify all translatable strings within the shipped configuration.

The secondary reason is to provide actual translation forms for configuration based on your data and to expose translatable configuration pieces to external tools.

Each module can have as many configuration the `.yml` files as needed. All of these are explained in one or more schema files that are shipped with the module. As a simple example of how schema files work, let's look at the system's maintenance settings in the `system.maintenance.yml` file at `core/modules/system/config/install`. The file's contents are as follows:

```
message: '@site is currently under maintenance. We should be back
shortly. Thank you for your patience.'
langcode: en
```

The `system` module's schema files live in `core/modules/system/config/schema`. These define the basic types but, for our example, the most important aspect is that they define the schema for the maintenance settings. The corresponding schema section from the `system.schema.yml` file is as follows:

```
system.maintenance:
  type: mapping
  label: 'Maintenance mode'
  mapping:
    message:
      type: text
      label: 'Message to display when in maintenance mode'
    langcode:
      type: string
      label: 'Default language'
```

The first line corresponds to the filename for the `.yml` file, and the nested lines underneath the first line describe the file's contents.

Mapping is a basic type for key-value pairs (always the top-level type in `.yml`). The `system.maintenance.yml` file is labeled as `label: 'Maintenance mode'`. Then, the actual elements in the mapping are listed under the `mapping` key. As shown in the code, the file has two items, so the `message` and `langcode` keys are described. These are a text and a string value, respectively. Both values are given a label as well in order to identify them in configuration forms.

Chapter 5, The Anatomy of Schema Files will cover schema files in greater detail.

Learning the difference between active and staging directories

By now, you know that Drupal works with the two directories `active` and `staging`. But what is the intention behind those directories? And how do we use them?

The configuration used by your site is called the `active` configuration since it's the configuration that is affecting the site's behavior right now. The current (`active`) configuration is stored in the database and direct changes to your site's configuration go into the specific tables. The reason Drupal 8 stores the active configuration in the database is that it enhances performance and security. Source: `https://www.drupal.org/node/2241059`.

However, sometimes you might not want to store the active configuration in the database and might need to use a different storage mechanism. For example, using the filesystem as configuration storage will enable you to track changes in the site's configuration using a versioning system such as Git or SVN.

Changing the active configuration storage

If you do want to switch your active configuration storage to files, here's how:

 Note that changing the configuration storage is only possible before installing Drupal. After installing it, there is no way to switch to another configuration storage!

To use a different configuration storage mechanism, you have to make some modifications to your `settings.php` file.

First, you'll need to find the section named `Active configuration settings`. Now you will have to uncomment the line that starts with `$settings['bootstrap_config_storage']` to enable file-based configuration storage. Additionally, you need to copy the existing `default.services.yml` (next to your `settings.php` file) to a file named `services.yml` and enable the new configuration storage:

```
services:
  # Override configuration storage.
  config.storage:
    class: Drupal\Core\Config\CachedStorage
```

```
    arguments: ['@config.storage.active', '@cache.config']
config.storage.active:
    # Use file storage for active configuration.
    alias: config.storage.file
```

This tells Drupal to override the default service used for configuration storage and use `config.storage.file` as the active configuration storage mechanism instead of the default database storage.

After installing the site with these settings, we will take another look at the config directory in `sites/default/files` (assuming you didn't change to the location of the `active` and `staging` directory):

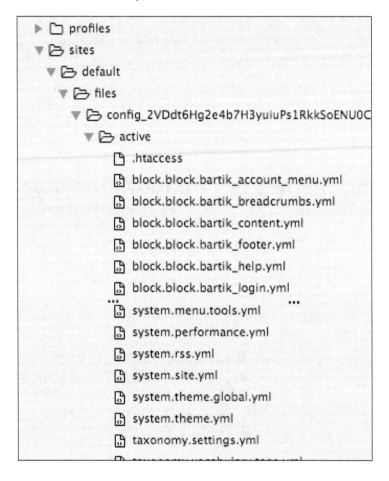

As you can see, the `active` directory contains the entire site's configuration. The files in this directory get copied here during the website's installation process. Whenever you make a change to your website, the change is reflected in these files.

Exporting a configuration (as we did in the previous chapter) always exports a snapshot of the active configuration, regardless of the storage method.

The `staging` directory contains the changes you want to add to your site. Drupal compares the `staging` directory to the `active` directory and checks for changes between them. In the previous chapter, we taught you how to use the Configuration Management Interface to export and import configuration files. When you upload your compressed export file, it actually gets placed inside the `staging` directory.

This means you can save yourself the trouble of using the interface to export and import the compressed file if you're comfortable enough with copy-and-pasting files to another directory. Just make sure you copy all of the files to the `staging` directory even if only one of the files was changed. Any missing files are interpreted as deleted configuration, and will mess up your site.

In order to get the contents of `staging` into `active`, we simply have to use the synchronize option at `admin/config/development/configuration` again. This page will show us what was changed and allows us to import the changes. On importing, your active configuration will get overridden with the configuration in your `staging` directory. Note that the files inside the `staging` directory will not be removed after the synchronization is finished. The next time you want to copy-and-paste from your `active` directory, make sure you empty `staging` first.

Note that you cannot override files directly in the active directory. The changes have to be made inside staging and then synchronized.

Changing the storage location of the active and staging directories

In case you do not want Drupal to store your configuration in `sites/default/files`, you can set the path according to your wishes. Actually, this is recommended for security reasons, as these directories should never be accessible over the Web or by unauthorized users on your server.

Additionally, it makes your life easier if you work with version control. By default, the whole `files` directory is usually ignored in version-controlled environments because Drupal writes to it, and having the `active` and `staging` directory located within `sites/default/files` would result in them being ignored too.

So how do we change the location of the configuration directories?

Before installing Drupal, you will need to create and modify the `settings.php` file that Drupal uses to load its basic configuration data from (that is, the database connection settings). If you haven't done it yet, copy the `default.settings.php` file and rename the copy to `settings.php`. Afterwards, open the new file with the editor of your choice and search for the following line:

```
$config_directories = array();
```

Change the preceding line to the following (or simply insert your addition at the bottom of the file).

```
$config_directories = array(
  CONFIG_ACTIVE_DIRECTORY => './../config/active', // folder outside
the webroot
  CONFIG_STAGING_DIRECTORY => './../config/staging', // folder outside
the webroot
);
```

The directory names can be chosen freely, but it is recommended that you at least use similar names to the default ones so that you or other developers don't get confused when looking at them later. Remember to put these directories outside your webroot, or at least protect the directories using an `.htaccess` file (if using Apache as the server).

Directly after adding the paths to your `settings.php` file, make sure you remove write permissions from the file as it would be a security risk if someone could change it. Drupal will now use your custom location for its configuration files on installation.

You can also change the location of the configuration directories after installing Drupal. Open up your `settings.php` file and find these two lines near the end of the file and start with `$config_directories`. Change their paths to something like this:

$config_directories['active'] = './../config/active';

$config_directories['staging] = './../config/staging';

This path places the directories above your Drupal root.

Now that you know about active and staging, let's learn more about the different types of configuration you can create on your own.

Simple configuration versus configuration entities

As soon as you want to start storing your own configuration, you need to understand the differences between simple configuration and configuration entities. Here's a short definition of the two types of configuration used in Drupal. Please refer to the next chapter for an in-depth look at the Configuration Management API to learn more about these two.

Simple configuration

This configuration type is easier to implement and therefore ideal for basic configuration settings that result in Boolean values, integers, or simple strings of text being stored, as well as global variables that are used throughout your site. A good example would be the value of an on/off toggle for a specific feature in your module, or our previously used example of the site name configured by the system module:

```
name: 'Configuration Management in Drupal 8'
```

Simple configuration also includes any settings that your module requires in order to operate correctly. For example, JavaScript aggregation has to be either on or off. If it doesn't exist, the system module won't be able to determine the appropriate course of action.

Configuration entities

Configuration entities are much more complicated to implement but far more flexible. They are used to store information about objects that users can create and destroy without breaking the code. A good example of configuration entities is an image style provided by the image module.

Take a look at the `image.style.thumbnail.yml` file:

```
uuid: fe1fba86-862c-49c2-bf00-c5e1f78a0f6c
langcode: en
status: true
dependencies: {   }
name: thumbnail
label: 'Thumbnail (100×100)'
effects:
  1cfec298-8620-4749-b100-ccb6c4500779:
    uuid: 1cfec298-8620-4749-b100-ccb6c4500779
```

```
      id: image_scale
      weight: 0
      data:
        width: 100
        height: 100
        upscale: false
  third_party_settings: {  }
```

This defines a specific style for images, so the system is able to create derivatives of images that a user uploads to the site.

Configuration entities also come with a complete set of create, read, update, and delete (CRUD) hooks that are fired just like any other entity in Drupal, making them an ideal candidate for configuration that might need to be manipulated or responded to by other modules. As an example, the Views module uses configuration entities that allow for a scenario where, at runtime, hooks are fired that allow any other module to provide configuration (in this case, custom views) to the Views module.

Summary

In this chapter, you learned about how to store configuration and briefly got to know the two different types of configuration.

The next chapter will give you an in-depth look at the Configuration API.

4
The Configuration Management API

In the previous chapters, we explained the basic concepts of Configuration Management in Drupal 8 and also talked about the different types of configuration. Now we will get our hands dirty and learn about the Configuration Management API of Drupal 8. Here, we will dive into the Simple Configuration API and learn how configuration can be overridden. Later, we will take a closer look at how to create custom configuration entity types, and you'll also learn about the configuration's context system.

A simple configuration API

As you learned earlier in this book, there are several types of configuration objects in Drupal 8: simple configuration and the more complex configuration entities.

Working with configuration data

If you've worked with Drupal 7 before and have written some custom code, you will surely remember the variable subsystem. Drupal 7 itself and many modules store their settings in the {variable} database table. Every configuration saved to this table needs to be serialized before saving and converted back to its original state while reading from the table. To read and write configuration, Drupal 7 has the widely used functions variable_get($name) and variable_set($name, $value).

Here are some small examples of how Drupal 7 reads and saves simple configuration settings, taken from `system.admin.inc`:

```php
<?php
// The status message depends on whether an admin theme is currently
in use:
// a value of 0 means the admin theme is set to be the default theme.
$admin_theme = variable_get('admin_theme', 0);
...
// Set the default theme.
variable_set('theme_default', $theme);
?>
```

As you can see, Drupal 7 makes it quite simple to access the site settings and permanently save them back to the database table.

However, in Drupal 8, all of this changes. The complete variable subsystem has been removed from the Drupal core and is reborn as the Simple Configuration API.

The preceding example looks slightly different in Drupal 8:

```php
<?php
// The status message depends on whether an admin theme is currently
in use:
// a value of 0 means the admin theme is set to be the default theme.
$admin_theme = \Drupal::config('system.theme')->get('admin');
...
// Set the default theme.
\Drupal::configFactory()->getEditable('system.theme')
  ->set('default', $theme)
  ->save();
?>
```

Pretty simple, right?

Let's take a closer look at the single elements of the function calls.

Retrieving the configuration object

Drupal 8 was built on top of the Symfony framework to make use of its code base while not having to reinvent the wheel. Additionally, Drupal 8 switched to object-oriented code, so it mainly uses classes instead of procedural code within the core components. To make it easier to move away from procedural to object-orientated code, the generic class `Drupal` has been created.

Calling \Drupal acts as a global accessor to services within the complete system. Using this notation, you can easily access the basic services such as caching the database, the language manager, or configuration. For example, \Drupal::config($name) is a shortcut for the function get($name) of the ConfigFactory service, so you don't need to initialize the complete service every time you would like to load a configuration object. The function is the main entry point to the Configuration Management API, so there is no way around it when reading the configuration.

Our example simply returns the configuration object for the name system.theme. Do you still remember the .yml files we used as an example in previous chapters? The name sounds familiar, right? In fact, a file named system.theme.yml exists in the config directory of the system module:

```
admin: ''
default: stark
```

So \Drupal::config('system.theme') will allow us to access the configuration stored in this file.

Getting configuration values

The next part of the call is ->get('admin'). Using this function allows us to access a single value of the loaded configuration object. In this case, the call retrieves the value of admin key that our configuration object stored in system.theme.yml.

Of course, configuration values can be nested as well. Looking at system.theme.global.yml as an example, we see a small hierarchy of configuration with mimetype and path being children of the key favicon:

```
favicon:
  mimetype: image/vnd.microsoft.icon
  path: ''
  url: ''
  use_default: true
```

In order to access the value of the configuration, Drupal offers a few different options. The first option is to directly get the value. To do this, we need to merge the keys of each parent configuration with the one we would like to read, starting from the highest level. The key needs to be separated by a single dot, so the merged key for our (nested) example would be favicon.mimetype, and the complete call would be $value = \Drupal::config('system.theme.global')->get('favicon.mimetype');. The $value parameter now contains the string image/vnd.microsoft.icon.

Alternatively, you could simply use `$value = \Drupal::config('system.theme.global')->get('favicon');` to read all children of the top-level key `favicon`. Using this call, `$value` will hold an associative array that contains all child configurations of the key "favicon" in `system.theme.global.yml`:

```php
<?php
array(
  'mimetype' => 'image/vnd.microsoft.icon',
  'path' => '',
  'url' => '',
  'use_defaults' => TRUE,
);
?>
```

It is also possible to completely omit the configuration name `$value = \Drupal::config('system.theme.global')->get()`. Now, `$value` holds an array with the complete configuration object stored in `system.theme.global`.

Setting configuration values

The `set` function call is basically the same as `\Drupal::config($name)->get($name);` with one minor but important difference: you are not able to change configuration values you received using `get($name)`. To update configuration objects, you need to retrieve them using the function `getEditable($name)` of the configuration factory. Therefore, we do not use the shortcut `\Drupal::config('system.theme')`, but need to load the configuration object using `\Drupal::configFactory()->getEditable('system.theme')`. Trying to change the value of a configuration object loaded using the `::config()` shortcut or `get($name)` will result in an exception.

If the key you are using with `set()` doesn't exist yet in the configuration object, it will be added so we can use it later.

Let's get back to our earlier example. We override the configuration object `system.theme` and set the default theme to the value of the variable `$theme`. The value isn't saved permanently yet; only the current instance of the editable loaded configuration object has been modified. To write the changed values back into the configuration object (depending on your configuration storage mechanism, this would be in the database, in `system.theme.yml`, or in something else), we need to do a call to the `save()` function on the configuration object.

This function validates the values of the modified configuration object against a possibly existing schema and writes the configuration object back to the active storage.

When setting values of a configuration object, you are not limited to one value per call. If you would like to set several values at once, you need to provide an array with all keys and values to set or add:

```php
<?php
// Set multiple configuration values at once.
\Drupal::configFactory()->getEditable('system.theme')->set(array(
  'admin' => 'my_admin_theme',
  'default' => 'my_custom_theme',
))->save();
?>
```

In this example code, we update the values of the current admin theme and change the value for the default theme.

It is also possible to replace all data of a configuration object. If you want to do this, use the `setData($data)` function. The `$data` parameter must contain every key and value pair that a call to `get()` (without a name specified) would return. If you accidently miss a key, the key and its value will be removed from the active configuration, which might break your site (depending on the configuration you are updating). Setting single configuration values is not possible with this function. You need to call `set($name, $value)` multiple times.

Removing configuration values

Sometimes, you need to remove configuration values from a configuration object on purpose. Back in Drupal 7, you could do this very easily using `variable_del($name)`. Drupal 8 offers two functions to remove configuration, `clear($key)` and `delete()`:

```php
<?php
// Load configuration object.
$config = \Drupal::configFactory()->getEditable('system.theme');
// Remove single value from configuration object.
$config->clear('admin')->save();
$admin_theme = \Drupal::config('system.theme')->get('admin');
?>
```

As you can see, we also need to save the changes so that the modified configuration object gets written to the corresponding file. The variable `$admin_theme` in the preceding example will hold the value NULL, since we removed it from the configuration object.

To remove entire configuration objects, you need to use the `delete()` function:

```php
<?php
// Load configuration object.
$config = \Drupal::configFactory()->getEditable('system.theme');
// Remove entire configuration object.
$config->delete();
$theme_default = \Drupal::config('system.theme')->get('default');
?>
```

The `delete()` function should not be followed by a call to `save()` since this would result in an empty configuration file that could break your site.

Executing the code would set the value of the `$theme_default` variable to NULL because the configuration object itself no longer exists.

Best practices

If you plan to do several function calls on the same configuration object, do not instantiate the same object multiple times. The following code is an example of what not to do:

```php
<?php
\Drupal::configFactory()->getEditable('system.theme')->set('admin',
'seven')->save();
\Drupal::configFactory()->getEditable('system.theme')->set('default',
'bartik')->save();
?>
```

This code has to load the configuration object `system-theme` multiple times and (even worse) needs to write the entire configuration object to the configuration storage for every change you have made.

A much better solution is to instantiate the configuration object only once and save it to a variable. This variable can then be used to modify the object and save all changes at once:

```php
<?php
// Load the editable configuration object.
$config = \Drupal::configFactory->getEditable('system.theme');
// Set value of first configuration item.
$config->set('admin', 'seven');
// Set another value.
$config->set('default', 'bartik');
```

```
// Save changes back to configuration storage.
$config->save();
?>
```

Getting notified about configuration changes

Whenever Drupal saves or deletes a configuration object, it sends out a notification about it. Thanks to Symfony's event listener system, modules can listen to these events and react to the changes.

Creating a class that implements `EventSubscriberInterface` is the first thing you need to do when writing a custom module that you want to react when a configuration object is saved or deleted.

In the following examples, we create a module named `cm_example`, so we start with a basic `cm_example.info.yml`:

```
name: Configuration Management example
type: module
description: 'Example for Configuration Management in Drupal 8.'
package: Custom
version: 8.x-0.1
core: 8.x
```

To register our event subscriber, a file named `cm_example.services.yml` needs to be created with the following contents:

```
services:
  cm_example.config_subscriber:
    class: Drupal\cm_example\EventSubscriber\ConfigSubscriber
    tags:
      - { name: event_subscriber }
```

Without this file and definition, Drupal will have no idea whether we would like to react on any event it triggers.

Next, we need to create an implementation of the previously mentioned
`EventSubscriberInterface` to create a custom reaction on configuration changes.
We put this file in the `src/EventSubscriber` folder of our module directory:

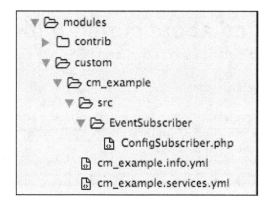

The source code in the ConfigSubscriber.php is as follows:

```php
<?php
/**
 * @file
 * Contains \Drupal\cm_example\EventSubscriber\ConfigSubscriber.
 */

namespace Drupal\cm_example\EventSubscriber;

use Drupal\Core\Config\ConfigCrudEvent;
use Drupal\Core\Config\ConfigEvents;
use Symfony\Component\EventDispatcher\EventSubscriberInterface;

/**
 * Custom config subscriber.
 */
class ConfigSubscriber implements EventSubscriberInterface {

  /**
   * {@inheritdoc}
   */
  static function getSubscribedEvents() {
    $events[ConfigEvents::SAVE][] = array('onConfigSave', 40);
    return $events;
```

```
    }

    /**
     * React on changes of the configuration object "system.theme".
     *
     * @param ConfigCrudEvent $event
     *    The configuration event.
     */
    public function onConfigSave(ConfigCrudEvent $event) {
      $saved_config = $event->getConfig();
      if ($saved_config->getName() == 'system.theme') {
        // Do some magic based on the saved configuration.
      }
    }
  }
  ?>
```

In the `getSubscribedEvents()` function, we create a list of all events that we would like to react on. This is not limited to configuration events as shown in the preceding code; you can even react to basic kernel events, that is, `KernelEvents::REQUEST`, which occurs at the very beginning of request dispatching. In our example, we register a custom function named `onConfigSave` to the event `ConfigEvents::SAVE`.

To allow prioritization of all registered functions, we add a weight to the call. The functions are executed in the order of their priority, so the function with the highest priority will be executed first. Make sure you don't set the weight to a value greater than 255, as this is the weight of the functions that the basic `ConfigFactory` uses. A value between 0 and 40 should fit all your needs.

If you now save a configuration object on your site, the `onConfigSave()` function in our custom class is called. Within the function, we have access to the configuration object that has been written to the configured storage.

As said before, you are not limited to configuration events. With `EventSubscriberInterface`, it is also possible to override the configuration.

Overriding the configuration

While working with your site, you sometimes need to override the configuration. Looking back at Drupal 7, we remember it was possible to set variables in the settings.php file. It had the global $conf variable in which you could simply override the existing configuration. For example, you could set the configuration for the contrib module Environment indicator (https://drupal.org/project/environment_indicator) directly in the settings.php file:

```php
<?php
// Develop environment.
$conf['environment_indicator_overwritten_name'] = 'develop';
$conf['environment_indicator_overwritten_color'] = '#ff940f';
?>
```

Though this is very handy, a huge drawback of this system is that it directly changes the current configuration. Submitting a settings form that also contains this configuration might save the overridden values to the database, which we don't usually want.

Drupal 8 introduces a completely new configuration override system where the overridden configuration is a new layer on top of the standard configuration values. Configuration forms do not display the overridden data, so they won't pollute the active configuration storage. With the new system, it is even possible to store the overridden configuration with other configurations to support version control. This is very useful for maintaining language-specific overrides (as explained later) in single files.

Drupal 8 introduces three different types of configuration overrides:

* Global overrides
* Language overrides
* Module overrides

Global overrides

The simple global $conf system known from Drupal 7 is retained (while renaming the variable to $config), and therefore it is still possible to globally override specific configuration values using the file settings.php. None of the values changed here are visible in the Drupal administration interface, so you don't have to worry about overwriting the (possibly version-controlled) active configuration with these overrides.

Every time you retrieve a configuration value using \Drupal::config($name)->get($name), which we described earlier in this chapter, the global $config system is capable of changing the returned value:

```php
<?php
// Get system site maintenance message text. This value may be overridden by
// default from global $config (as well as translations, see below).
$message = \Drupal::config('system.maintenance')->get('message');
?>
```

Using \Drupal::configFactory()->getEditable($name)->get($name) instead will return the configuration's value without any overrides.

To override the maintenance message, you could add the following code to your settings.php:

```php
<?php
$config['system.maintenance']['message'] = 'Sorry, our site is currently down.';
?>
```

When putting your site in maintenance mode, it will display the text configured in the settings.php file instead of displaying the default message from system.maintenance.yml.

As you can see, you only have to reference the name and the keys of the configuration object to change its value.

 Not all configuration values are overridable using $config. For example, the list of installed modules could not be overridden here because the installation process would not be triggered.

Apart from the global $config system, there is also the global $settings system:

```php
<?php
// Set a custom theme for offline pages.
$settings['maintenance_theme'] = 'my_custom_maintenance_theme';
?>
```

However, this setting is not defined as a configuration object (hence, it misses the dot-notation). Unlike $config, $settings contains a configuration that cannot be changed or removed programmatically. Some of the configuration (that is, the database settings) stored in $settings are required in a very early phase of the Drupal bootstrap, when even the configuration system is not available yet, so it is kept away from $config.

To access the configuration of $settings in a module, you need to use the settings() function instead of the previously described \Drupal::config():

```php
<?php
use \Drupal\Core\Site\Settings;
// Load name of maintenance theme.
$theme = Settings::get()->get('maintenance_theme','bartik');
?>
```

The \Drupal\Core\Site\Settings class utilizes only a few functions whereas you will mainly use get($name, $default) to retrieve single read-only settings.

Language overrides

Apart from the possibility of overriding configuration using global $config and global $settings in the settings.php, there is also a language override system within the ConfigFactory.

For example, to set the current language for the current configuration, the language module defines an event subscriber class named LanguageRequestSubscriber that overrides the current language used by the ConfigFactory on every page request using the EventSubscriberInterface we've learned about earlier.

When loading a configuration object from storage, ConfigFactory is now able to load configuration data specific to the current language from the configuration storage. The language overrides are stored right next to the normal configuration. The only this is different from the default configuration files is the naming.

Using the default storage-mechanism-translated configuration, the translation is identified additionally by a collection; that is, translating your site's name to German will add a new entry to table {config}, where the column collection is filled with the language.de string.

If you use file-based storage for your configuration, you will notice a folder named `language` within your configuration directory. This directory contains one directory per language and includes all files of the translated configuration. In a custom module, you can also add custom translations. Simply add a `language` directory to your `config/install`, as shown in the following screenshot:

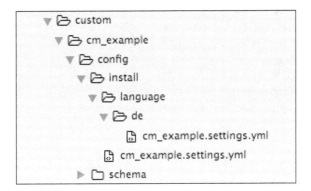

For every language for which you would like to provide translations, add another directory under `language` using the language code as the name (that is, `de` for German or `hu` for Hungarian). Then, place the configuration files you would like to translate in these directories and translate the values.

> Translating configuration values provided by other modules that use them is not recommended. If the configuration translation already exists, your module will not be installed.

Only put the configuration you translate in these files; that is, if you would like to translate only the name of your site to German, create a file named `system.site.yml` in the directory `config/install/language/de` (as shown in the preceding image) and put the following contents in it:

```
name: 'Konfigurationsmanagement in Drupal 8'
```

During installation of your module, the translation is imported into Drupal and is directly available on your site.

For some tasks, it is necessary to load configuration objects in a language other than the current site language. For example, think of sending e-mails to various users in different languages. The e-mails should be sent in the user's language and not in the site's language.

To get configuration values in the correct language, you need to set the configuration's override language:

```php
<?php
// Retrieve the current user object.
$account = \Drupal::currentUser();
// Get the language manager.
$language_manager = \Drupal::languageManager();
// Load preferred user language.
$language = \Drupal::languageManager()->getLanguage($account-
>getPreferredLangcode());
// Set configuration language override.
$language_manager->setConfigOverrideLanguage($language);
?>
```

From now on, Drupal will return configuration values in the requested language if there were overrides available for the requested values.

If you need to switch the configuration language, it is useful to remember the current language first before setting a new one. This way, you can switch back to the original language after working with the translated configuration values:

```php
<?php
// Store original language.
$language_original = $language_manager->getConfigOverrideLanguage();
// Set configuration language override.
$language_manager->setConfigOverrideLanguage($language);
// Do some stuff, i.e. send localized emails.
// ...
// Set the language back to its original value.
$language_manager->setConfigOverrideLanguage($language_original);
?>
```

Module overrides

The last type of configuration override is the module override. While Drupal core handles global overrides as well as language overrides, there are many other use cases for different kinds of overrides. Think of a configuration override based on the roles a user has, the current domain, and so on. The possibilities are nearly endless.

Say you would like to override the name of your site using a custom module. First, you need to extend the `services.yml` file we used in a previous example with these lines (adapt them to your needs and replace `cm_example` with the name of your module):

```
cm_example.config_factory_override:
  class: Drupal\cm_example\Config\ExampleConfigFactoryOverride
  arguments: ['@config.storage', '@event_dispatcher', '@config.
typed']
  tags:
    - { name: config.factory.override, priority: 10 }
```

As you can see, we define a new service using the `ExampleConfigFactoryOverride` class. The key part here is the `tags` section; with the name `config.factory.override`, you tell Drupal that there is a new service that wants to override the configuration factory. We give the service a priority of 10, so it is executed after most default services in the queue (that is, the language override has a very low priority to execute it as one of the first services).

Next, we create the class itself in a directory named `Config` under the `src` directory of our custom module:

```php
<?php

/**
 * @file
 * Contains \Drupal\cm_example\Config\ExampleConfigFactoryOverride.
 */

namespace Drupal\cm_example\Config;

use Drupal\Core\Config\ConfigFactoryOverrideInterface;
use Drupal\Core\Config\StorageInterface;

/**
 * Provides custom overrides for the configuration factory.
 */
class ExampleConfigFactoryOverride implements
ConfigFactoryOverrideInterface {

  /**
   * {@inheritdoc}
   */
  public function loadOverrides($names) {
    $overrides = array();
```

```
      if (in_array('system.site', $names)) {
        $overrides['system.site'] = ['name' => 'Customized site name'];
      }
      return $overrides;
    }

    /**
     * {@inheritdoc}
     */
    public function getCacheSuffix() {
      return 'CmExampleConfigOverrider';
    }

    /**
     * {@inheritdoc}
     */
    public function createConfigObject($name, $collection =
  StorageInterface::DEFAULT_COLLECTION) {
      return NULL;
    }

  }
  ?>
```

The class simply implements `ConfigFactoryOverrideInterface` and implements the three `loadOverrides()`, `getCacheSuffix()`, and `createConfigObject()` functions.

You do not need to worry about the latter ones because the main function needed for our purpose is `loadOverrides()`. In our example, the function simply checks whether `system.site` is one of the configuration keys `ConfigFactory` collects overrides for, and returns a list of overrides for this configuration object.

If multiple modules registered a custom configuration override service, the service with the highest priority within all module overrides will be called last; so, if multiple services override the same configuration object, the last one is used for the override and provides the current value.

Across the different types of configuration overrides, language overrides have the lowest priority. Module overrides takes precedence over language overrides, and are overridden themselves by overrides of the `global $config` and `global $settings` systems.

Avoiding overrides

When writing a custom configuration form, it is very useful to get the configuration objects without overrides. Otherwise, the overridden configuration will get into the saved configuration. As for localized configuration, you'll never want to override the original configuration with localized values.

To get configuration values without any overrides, Drupal provides the function getEditable() of ConfigFactory. While configuration objects returned by get() are immutable, getEditable() returns configuration objects that may be changed.

When inheriting your form class from the core ConfigFormBase class, you can simply implement the getEditableConfigNames() function, and return a list of all the names of the configuration objects your form might alter:

```php
<?php
/**
 * @file
 * Contains \Drupal\cm_example\Form\ExampleConfigurationForm.
 */

namespace Drupal\cm_example\Form;

use Drupal\Core\Form\ConfigFormBase;
use Drupal\Core\Form\FormStateInterface;

/**
 * Provides the site configuration form.
 */
class ExampleConfigurationForm extends ConfigFormBase {

  /**
   * {@inheritdoc}
   */
  public function getFormId() {
    return 'example_configuration_form';
  }

  /**
   * {@inheritdoc}
   */
  protected function getEditableConfigNames() {
```

```
        return ['cm_example.settings'];
    }
}
?>
```

You are then able to load the configuration object using `$this->config($name)` and change the configuration value. Drupal will automatically load the configuration object without overrides if the name is in the list returned by `getEditableConfigNames()`, so you don't have to bother about this.

Creating configuration entity types

In *Chapter 3, Drupal 8's Take on Configuration Management*, we learned about the different types of configuration: simple configuration and configuration entities. Though Drupal 8 comes with several different configuration entity types, it is sometimes useful to create your own configuration entity type when developing a custom module.

Adding the basics

At first, we need to create a simple interface for the new configuration entity type. This class must extend the generic `ConfigEntityInterface` class, which is common for all configuration entities:

```php
<?php
/**
 * @file
 * Contains \Drupal\cm_example\CmExampleInterface.
 */

namespace Drupal\cm_example\Entity;

use Drupal\Core\Config\Entity\ConfigEntityInterface;

/**
 * Provides an interface defining an Example entity.
 */
interface CmExampleInterface extends ConfigEntityInterface {
  // Add getter and setter methods for your configuration properties
  here.
}
?>
```

If you would like to add some specific getter and setter functions for properties used by your configuration entity, you will need to do this here as well.

Next, we need to add the main configuration entity class that handles all the stuff you would like to do with the configuration data. To avoid writing too much code and re-inventing everything, you should simply extend the core class `ConfigEntityBase`. This will give you a large set of functions to handle your configuration entity so that you don't need to bother with this.

The most important thing in the main class is the comment block right above the class definition, the so-called `Annotation`, by which the main definition of the type is done.

 Annotations are meta-information used to describe classes, properties, and functions, and are always put in comments above the described structure. If you have written code for Drupal before, you will certainly know @param or @return for functions; these are annotations used by parsers that create documentation.

To tell Drupal about your custom configuration entity type, you will need to add the `@ConfigEntityType` annotation to your class comment:

```php
<?php

/**
 * @file
 * Definition of Drupal\cm_example\Entity\CmExample.
 */

namespace Drupal\cm_example\Entity;

use Drupal\cm_example\CmExampleInterface;
use Drupal\Core\Config\Entity\ConfigEntityBase;

/**
 * Defines the CmExample configuration entity.
 *
 * @ConfigEntityType(
 *   id = "cm_example",
 *   label = @Translation("CM Example"),
 *   handlers = {
 *     "form" = {
```

```
 *          "delete" = "Drupal\Core\Entity\EntityDeleteForm"
 *        },
 *      "list_builder" = "Drupal\cm_example\CmExampleListBuilder",
 *      },
 *    config_prefix = "cm_example",
 *    admin_permission = "administer site configuration",
 *    entity_keys = {
 *      "id" = "id",
 *      "label" = "label",
 *      },
 *    links = {
 *        "edit-form" = "/admin/structure/cm_example/manage/{cm_
example}",
 *        "delete-form" = "/admin/structure/cm_example/manage/{cm_
example}/delete",
 *        "collection" = "/admin/structure/cm_example",
 *      }
 *  )
 */
class CmExample extends ConfigEntityBase implements CmExampleInterface
{

  /**
   * The machine name for the configuration entity.
   *
   * @var string
   */
  protected $id;

  /**
   * The human-readable name of the configuration entity.
   *
   * @var string
   */
  public $label;

}
?>
```

Within this class annotation, you define the internal name and the label for the new configuration entity type. Additionally, you may define the handlers used to display and store entities of the new type and the paths for different tasks on the entity (that is, the edit form).

Taking control of your data

Since we didn't define custom handlers for storage, listing, and access control, Drupal will use the default handlers for these tasks. You can easily use your own handlers: simply add `storage`, `list_builder`, or `access` to the handler array within the annotation, and set the names of the appropriate classes.

For example, a custom access handler should extend the basic `EntityAccessControlHandler` class and override the `checkAccess()` function.

 For an in-depth example on how to create a custom configuration entity type and the different handlers and form classes, look at the great `Examples` module (`https://www.drupal.org/project/examples`).

Summary

After defining all the classes that we need in order to add, edit, and list entities of the new configuration entity type, we are now able to use this type in configuration objects like every other core type.

So what did we learn in this chapter? We learned about how to get and update configuration values and about the different ways of overriding configuration provided by Drupal or modules; then we created a very simple configuration entity type. Thus, by now, you should be able to create a module and manage your custom configuration right away.

5

The Anatomy of
Schema Files

In the previous chapters, we learned about the fundamental principles of Drupal 8's Configuration Management, and took a look at the Configuration Management API. So we now know how to work with configuration objects and how to read and write individual configuration.

However, how does Drupal validate data within a site's configuration? We probably need a setting to accept integer values or a URI. Or we would like to enforce fixed structure in our configuration data. This is exactly where schema files come into play.

This chapter will tell you about schema files and how Drupal uses them for Configuration Management. We will learn about the structure of schema files used by Drupal and how you can write your own schema for custom configuration.

What are schema files in Drupal?

With schema files, you can describe the contents of a configuration file. You can determine which configuration keys are allowed in a specific configuration object and which data type configuration data needs to have. Drupal 8's schema files are inspired by *Kwalify*.

 Kwalify (`http://www.kuwata-lab.com/kwalify/`) is a parser and schema validator for YAML and JSON. It adds a schema to YAML and JSON as, for example DTD does for XML.

The format used by *Kwalify* was slightly modified to fit the needs of the structure needed in Drupal 8 but, generally, it is largely identical.

Schema files were not introduced for validation purposes only. The primary use case for schema files was to support multilingual configuration in Drupal 8. It was necessary to create a tool to identify all translatable strings within the configuration files, so the entire configuration, views, menu items, and user roles that you may define in a custom module or theme could be offered as translation packages on `http://localize.drupal.org`.

The second very important use case for schema files is forms that translate configuration data. Without schema files, it would be very hard for Drupal to display configuration values in the expected type or to discover whether a configuration value is valid. Drupal automatically typecasts configuration values to the type defined in the corresponding schema in order to ensure the right data type is used when the configuration is saved.

Additionally, Drupal has nearly no chance of printing out the human-readable name for the form element of a configuration element just by looking at the configuration file.

Let's look at `system.file.yml` as an example:

```
allow_insecure_uploads: false
default_scheme: 'public'
path:
  temporary: ''
temporary_maximum_age: 21600
```

To use the intended data types while building the related form for this configuration object, Drupal needs to know which type of data to display and in to which type to save the values.

This information is precisely defined in the associated schema file.

The structure of a schema file

Schema files are located in a subdirectory of the `config` directory of each module that defines its own configuration. The name of this directory is `schema` (not very surprising, is it?). The schema files themselves are named after the module that defines the schema, followed by an optional identifier and the string `.schema.yml`. Again, using the system module as an example, the path to its schema file is `system/config/schema/system.schema.yml`.

Within each schema file, the top-level key corresponds to the name of the configuration file, the name of the configuration object that the schema should apply to. The following nested values describe the exact structure of the related configuration object.

Let's look at a part of the `system.schema.yml` for an explanation:

```
system.file:
  type: mapping
  label: 'File system'
  mapping:
    allow_insecure_uploads:
      type: boolean
      label: 'Allow insecure uploads'
    default_scheme:
      type: string
      label: 'Default download method'
    path:
      type: mapping
      label: 'Path settings'
      mapping:
        temporary:
          type: string
          label: 'Temporary directory'
    temporary_maximum_age:
      type: integer
      label: 'Maximum age for temporary files'
```

As mentioned before, the top-level key `system.file` references the configuration file `system.file.yml`, so the contents listed under this key define the content of the configuration object `system.file`.

The next lines in our example define the data types used for the values of the configuration data. We will explain the displayed schema in the next part of this chapter.

Properties

In the previous example, you see some of the properties used in schema files. These properties define the basic structure of the schema and influence the possible usage of the inherited configuration objects. Let's take a look at them:

- `type`: This is the data type of the configuration value. This may be either one of the base types or a derived type. We will show the difference between both later in this chapter.

- `label`: This is a short description for the value. It does not have to match a corresponding configuration form label but, for clarity, they should match.

- `translatable`: This indicates whether the defined data type is translatable or not.

- `translation context`: This is a string context used for the translation. Drupal uses different contexts to allow translating the same word depending on where it is used on the site. For example, the word `View` can be used either to describe a list of entities or simply to display something. The translation context helps to differentiate between both.

- `class`: This is used only on base types to define the class used to parse the data type. You don't have to worry about this normally.

- `mapping`: This type-specific property is used to list the underlying elements within a configuration element (for example, the children of `system.file` in the example shown before) as key-value pairs (like an associative array). Only strings are allowed for the keys of these key-value pairs.

- `sequence`: This is used to list the underlying elements within a sequence of values. In contrast to `mapping`, the keys in a sequence can be either integers or strings. You can think of the sequence as a simple indexed list.

Data types

Most of the basic types, as well as some more complex types, are defined in the `core.data_types.schema.yml` file:

```
# Basic scalar data types from typed data.
boolean:
  label: 'Boolean'
  class: '\Drupal\Core\TypedData\Plugin\DataType\Boolean'
email:
  label: 'Email'
  class: '\Drupal\Core\TypedData\Plugin\DataType\Email'
integer:
  label: 'Integer'
  class: '\Drupal\Core\TypedData\Plugin\DataType\Integer'
float:
  label: 'Float'
  class: '\Drupal\Core\TypedData\Plugin\DataType\Float'
string:
  label: 'String'
  class: '\Drupal\Core\TypedData\Plugin\DataType\String'
uri:
  label: 'Uri'
  class: '\Drupal\Core\TypedData\Plugin\DataType\Uri'
```

These types have a direct mapping to their Typed Data API counterparts. The Typed Data API has been created to provide developers with a consistent way to interact with data. By default, PHP is a very loosely-typed language. The Typed Data API is trying to fix this, so Drupal itself—or any another system on which you would like to expose your data—will not run into problems while guessing a value type. For example, using a configuration value of type `integer` will automatically cast the value to `int` in Drupal, so a developer who uses this value doesn't have to do this manually.

For configuration data, Drupal defines some additional types:

```
# Basic data types for configuration.
undefined:
  label: 'Undefined'
  class: '\Drupal\Core\Config\Schema\Undefined'
ignore:
  label: 'Ignore'
  class: '\Drupal\Core\Config\Schema\Ignore'
mapping:
  label: Mapping
  class: '\Drupal\Core\Config\Schema\Mapping'
  definition_class: '\Drupal\Core\TypedData\MapDataDefinition'
sequence:
  label: Sequence
  class: '\Drupal\Core\Config\Schema\Sequence'
  definition_class: '\Drupal\Core\TypedData\ListDataDefinition'
```

As mentioned before, `mapping` and `sequence` are basically the same, with mapping being similar to an associative array and sequence being similar to a simple indexed list.

On the other hand, setting the type of a configuration object to `undefined` equates to not defining a schema at all, so there is no point in using this type. When creating configuration data structures where no type is possible (for example, for testing purposes), you could use the `ignore` type. Elements of this type are not casted and always validate.

Reusing data types

In order to allow more flexibility and the reuse of data types, types can simply be derived from each other to create more complex data structures. For example, the type `label` is a simple extended data type that uses the basic data type `string` as its own type. In contrast to data of type `string`, the `label` type requires its data to be plain text and editable with a text field.

Sometimes, a module defines configuration using the same data structure from different places. For example, if you provide a configuration for e-mails, you always define the e-mail subject and the e-mail body. In your configuration, you can now write the following code in every configuration file that needs an `e-mail` configuration object:

```
cm_example.notification:
  type: mapping
  label: 'Notification settings'
  mapping:
    subject:
      type: label
      label: 'Subject'
    body:
      type: text
      label: 'Body'
```

Thanks to reusable data types, this can be covered in a single custom data type. This prevents errors in writing, and makes the structure of the configuration files much more readable:

```
# Mail text with subject and body parts.
mail:
  type: mapping
  label: 'Mail'
  mapping:
    subject:
      type: label
      label: 'Subject'
    body:
      type: text
      label: 'Body'
```

Whenever you need to reference an e-mail in your configuration, simply use `type: mail`, and Drupal automatically expands this to the complex type:

```
cm_example.notification:
  type: mapping
  label: 'Notification settings'
  mapping:
    email:
      type: mail
      label: 'Email'
```

Making data translatable

As shown before, there is also a `translatable` property for schema files. For example, the data type `label` makes use of it:

```
label:
  type: string
  label: 'Label'
  translatable: true
```

This property is the basic requirement for configuration data to be translated. Drupal is now able to identify the translatable configuration and create the correct forms and functions around it, so authorized users of the site may translate them. By default, only `label`, `text`, and `date_format` are built-in translatable data types.

Dynamic type references

As you can see from the previous examples, simple and complex data types are essential references to other data types. Sometimes, a type isn't fixed but depends on the data of the configuration object itself. Think of Drupal image styles. They can contain several different image effects, with each of the effects requiring a different structure. Let's look at the default configuration object of the image style `thumbnail` located in `image.style.thumbnail.yml`:

```
name: thumbnail
label: 'Thumbnail (100x100)'
effects:
  1cfec298-8620-4749-b100-ccb6c4500779:
    id: image_scale
    data:
      width: 100
      height: 100
      upscale: true
    weight: 0
    uuid: 1cfec298-8620-4749-b100-ccb6c4500779
langcode: en
```

Depending on the selected effect, the key `data` can contain a completely different structure. For example, the structure of the effect `image_crop` uses the property `anchor` instead of `upscale`. Here is an excerpt merely showing the image effect:

```
id: image_crop
data:
  width: 100
  height: 100
  anchor: 'top-left'
```

In order to map this dynamic data structure, we need to create a reference to the related data type by using the identifier of the image effect. Here's an excerpt from `image.schema.yml`:

```
image.style.*:
...
    effects:
      type: sequence
      sequence:
        type: mapping
          mapping:
            id:
              type: string
            data:
              type: image.effect.[%parent.id]
            weight:
              type: integer
            uuid:
              type: string
```

The schema excerpt shown here uses a dynamic type reference to name the data type for a single effect. Variable values used in data types should be enclosed in square brackets, and can be combined with fixed components (such as `image.effect.` in our example).

There are 3 types of dynamic references:

- Element-key references, for example, `[%key]`
- Sub-key references, such as `type: views.field.[plugin_id]`
- Parent-key references, such as `type: image.effect.[%parent.id]`

The element-key references

Taking `ckeditor.schema.yml` as an example, we have the following code:

```
plugins:
  type: sequence
  label: 'Plugins'
  sequence:
    type: ckeditor.plugin.[%key]
```

So, if you create a configuration object using `type: stylescombo` (stylescombo is a core style of the core `ckeditor` module), Drupal will automatically expand this to `ckeditor.plugin.stylescombo` and use the schema defined for this.

The sub-key references

The used data type is composed of the fixed part and the value of the property referenced by the sub-key. Let's take a look at the schema for filters in views:

```
filters:
  type: sequence
  label: 'Filters'
  sequence:
    type: views.filter.[plugin_id]
```

In a view, adding a filter for the node status (published/unpublished) will give you the following excerpt in the corresponding configuration object:

```
filters:
  status:
    field: status
    group: 1
    id: status
    table: node_field_data
    value: true
    plugin_id: boolean
    entity_type: node
    entity_field: status
```

Drupal now takes the value of the key `plugin_id` from the definition of the status filter and creates the type name from it. This results in the type `views.filter.boolean`, defined in `views.filter.schema.yml`.

The parent-key references

This creates a reference to the parent configuration object (the upper level in the hierarchy) and uses values from this object. For example, the `value` property of a view filter is forced to use `views.filter_value.[%parent.plugin_id]` as the type:

```
views_filter:
  type: views_handler
  mapping:
    operator:
      type: string
      label: 'Operator'
    value:
      type: views.filter_value.[%parent.plugin_id]
      label: 'Value'
```

Looking at the example from the sub-key reference, Drupal will take the plugin ID from the `status` filter and create the type for `value` from it, resulting in `views.filter_value.boolean`.

At first, this can be really confusing and hard to understand, but it allows maximum flexibility when creating dynamic configuration objects.

Coding standards

When developing for Drupal, it is not only a best practice to follow the Coding Standards for configuration (`https://www.drupal.org/coding-standards/config`), but it is also one of the things you need to internalize in your daily work. Of course, the Coding Standards do not apply to PHP only; there are even some guidelines for writing schema files.

The first rule of thumb is to simply follow the code style of the `.yml` files, as seen everywhere else in Drupal code. The key points are as follows:

- Add a comment to the file, explaining the purpose and the content of this file. If there is only one schema file in your module, you may use a comment such as `# Schema for the configuration files of the {YOURMODULENAME} module`.

- Do not use double quotes for strings; use single quotes whenever you need to wrap strings in quotes.

- Use single quotes for label values that have only one word, for consistency.

- Key definitions and types should never be put in quotes. According to the Drupal standard, key names and types must not contain spaces, so there is no need to wrap them in quotes.

- Integer values used in configuration data are casted to strings when written to the `.yml` files. Therefore, you need to wrap them in single quotes too.

- Avoid comments that provide no extra clarity to the schema. Each schema item needs to have a descriptive label anyway, so an additional comment may be superfluous for many items (for example, `Comment settings` above the section `comment.section`).

- Add labels at least to the translatable values and to their containers. Otherwise, the translation form for these values cannot be generated in a useful way (some elements in the form would lack labels).

- Use proper indentation so that you can easily see the structure within the schema (this is not a standard per se, but a best practice).

PHP API

Defining a schema for your configuration is not only for Drupal's internals, it may also help you while writing a custom module. For example, you might like to get the data type of a configuration object (say, for validation purposes or to print out information about the type).

In addition to the already known `\Drupal::config($name)` to load a single configuration object, there is `\Drupal::service('config.typed')`. Using this function, you can access the definition of a configuration object's data structure.

To load the type definition of, for example, `system.maintenance`, we could use the following code:

```php
<?php
$definition = \Drupal::service('config.typed')->getDefinition('system.
maintenance');
?>
```

This would result in an array that contains the following structure:

```php
<?php
$definition = array(
   'label' => 'Maintenance mode',
   'type' => 'system.maintenance',
   'class' => '\Drupal\Core\Config\Schema\Mapping',
   'definition_class' => '\Drupal\Core\TypedData\MapDataDefinition',
   'mapping' => array(
     'message' => array(
       'type' => 'text',
       'label' => 'Message to display when in maintenance mode',
     ),
     'langcode' => array(
       'type' => 'string',
       'label' => 'Default language',
     ),
   ),
);
?>
```

If we compare this with the definition of the configuration object `system.maintenance` in `system.schema.yml`, we will see that its values match:

```
system.maintenance:
  type: mapping
  label: 'Maintenance mode'
```

```
mapping:
  message:
    type: text
    label: 'Message to display when in maintenance mode'
  langcode:
    type: string
    label: 'Default language'
```

Retrieving the data for a single configuration item is as easy as getting the complete schema definition. You simply have to use `\Drupal::service('config.typed')->get($name)`. Depending on the structure of the configuration schema, you will probably have to chain multiple calls of `get()`.

For example, `\Drupal::service('config.typed')->get('system.maintenance')->get('message')->getDataDefinition()` will give you an array that holds the schema definition for the maintenance message. Later, you can access the properties of the definition and, for example, use them to create corresponding forms:

```
$message = \Drupal::service('config.typed')->get('system.
maintenance')->get('message')->getDataDefinition->toArray();
$label = $message['label'];
```

Even if it is theoretically possible to make changes to the configuration loaded using the Typed Data API, you shouldn't do this. Using `\Drupal::config()` is simpler and faster.

If you would like to inspect your configuration and learn more about the structure and how to generate forms based on a given configuration schema, you don't need to print out the information yourself; simply download and install the great Configuration inspector module (`https://drupal.org/project/config_inspector`). It will give you an overview of your configuration and help you while creating your configuration and the corresponding schema.

Summary

Schema files are required in order to define how configuration objects are structured and how (and if) Drupal should handle translation of configuration data. They are used to ensure that configuration data is loaded and saved in the correct data type, so developers don't need to worry about casting the values into the types they need.

If the data types provided by Drupal do not fit your needs, you can simply extend those types by creating your own.

With all this knowledge about configuration objects and configuration schemas, we will learn how to add configuration to custom modules in the next chapter.

6

Adding Configuration Management to Your Module

After we learned how to access configuration objects and how schema files are structured in previous chapters, you will surely want to know how to get all this fancy stuff into your shiny new module for Drupal 8.

We will learn how to include the default configuration in custom modules, how to define and use your own configuration, and how to create configuration forms.

Default configuration

Let's start with a simple task and add some default configuration to our example module.

In Drupal 7, you have to use custom code to create and update the default configuration, such as content types, views, or field configurations. Many people also use the great *Features* module that provides some handy functions to manage default configuration easily.

Drupal 8 uses the .yml files we talked about extensively in previous chapters to store information about the default configuration. The Configuration Management system itself takes care of creating and managing the default configuration, so we can focus on writing its definition rather than creating the functions for management.

An example

Let's add a custom vocabulary to our site and define the term container and its configuration in the example module we used in the previous chapters. The vocabulary should be named `Category` and have the internal identifier `cm_example_category` (this is the machine-readable name). For the vocabulary definition, we create a new file named `taxonomy.vocabulary.cm_example_news.yml` in the subdirectory called `config/install` of the module's main directory. To prevent conflicts with configuration provided by other modules, you should always respect the naming convention and prefix custom types (content types, vocabularies, and so on) with your module name followed by an underscore.

After creating the file, you can put the following code in it:

```
vid: cm_example_category
name: Category
description: 'List of categories'
status: true
hierarchy: 1
weight: 0
dependencies:
  enforced:
    module:
      - cm_example
langcode: en
```

As you can see, we simply define the basic configuration of the vocabulary, as we would do in the user interface as follows:

- The `vid` key is the unique identifier of the vocabulary (in the previous versions of Drupal, this was `vocabulary ID`, hence the name). To avoid name clashes with vocabularies created by other modules or by the administrator of the site, you should use your module's name as a prefix for this machine-readable identifier.

- The `name` and `description` keys hold the vocabulary's name and description that are visible in the user interface.

- Since we would like the vocabulary to be enabled and usable after installation, the value of the `status` key is set to `true`.

- In the `hierarchy` key, you can decide which type of hierarchy the new vocabulary should support:
  - ° This denotes that the hierarchy is disabled
  - ° This denotes a simple hierarchy (only 1 parent per term is allowed)
  - ° This denotes multiple parents (a term in this vocabulary can have multiple parents)

- To make sure the vocabulary is only available on the site as long as the defining module is installed, we declare a dependency to our module `cm_example` in the key `dependencies`. Using the `enforced` key, we tell Drupal to require this dependency regardless of the changes or the additions that a user of the site made to the configuration of the vocabulary.

 If you do not want to write the configuration manually, you can also create the vocabulary in the user interface and export the configuration using the configuration exporter on `admin/config/development/configuration/single/export`.

Of course, configuring the user interface and exporting it works will all types of configuration, whether defined by Drupal itself or other modules, so you can ship your module with predefined content types, views, user roles, block settings, or whatever needs to be configured to make your module work. A view, for example, would require you to create a file named `views.view.[name of your view].yml`, user roles would go into `user.role.[role name].yml`, and so on.

Remember to reinstall your module if you add a default configuration after installing the module since Drupal only imports configuration on installation of a module.

Defining and using your own configuration

Sometimes, including default configuration objects defined by other modules is not enough, and you may want to define your own configuration. As with many other parts of the Configuration Management in Drupal 8, this is not very complicated.

Setting your configuration file

Configuration files for configuration objects defined by a module reside in the `config/install` subdirectory of this module. In our example, this is `/modules/custom/cm_example/config/install`.

We put our example module in a directory named `custom` inside the `modules` directory to separate contributed modules downloaded from `https://drupal.org` from custom modules. This is a well-known best practice when creating sites to keep your modules organized.

In *Chapter 3, Drupal 8's take on Configuration Management*, we mentioned the naming conventions of configuration files. As said before, simple module settings should go into a file named `<module name>.settings.yml`; thus, in our case, we will name it `cm_example.settings.yml`:

```
items_per_page: 20
langcode: en
```

These settings will set the default language to `en` for English, and provide a simple setting named `items_per_page` in our module.

All settings saved to this file will define the default values for your module. Drupal will take these values on installation and use them as defaults unless overridden by the user or another module.

Of course, you are not limited to simple configuration in your module. If you need more complex configuration objects or configuration entities, this is also possible.

Custom configuration entity types

Let's take a look back at our custom configuration entity type named "CM Example", which we created in *Chapter 4, The Configuration Management API*:

```php
<?php
/**
 * @file
 * Definition of Drupal\cm_example\Entity\CmExample.
 */

namespace Drupal\cm_example\Entity;

use Drupal\cm_example\CmExampleInterface;
use Drupal\Core\Config\Entity\ConfigEntityBase;

/**
 * Defines the CmExample configuration entity.
 *
```

```
 * @ConfigEntityType(
 *   id = "cm_example",
 *   label = @Translation("CM Example"),
 *   handlers = {
 *     "form" = {
 *       "delete" = "Drupal\Core\Entity\EntityDeleteForm"
 *     },
 *     "list_builder" = "Drupal\cm_example\CmExampleListBuilder",
 *   },
 *   config_prefix = "cm_example",
 *   admin_permission = "administer site configuration",
 *   entity_keys = {
 *     "id" = "id",
 *     "label" = "label",
 *   },
 *   links = {
 *     "edit-form" = "/admin/structure/cm_example/manage/{cm_
example}",
 *     "delete-form" = "/admin/structure/cm_example/manage/{cm_
example}/delete",
 *     "collection" = "/admin/structure/cm_example",
 *   }
 * )
 */
class CmExample extends ConfigEntityBase implements CmExampleInterface
{

  /**
   * The machine name for the configuration entity.
   *
   * @var string
   */
  protected $id;

  /**
   * The human-readable name of the configuration entity.
   *
   * @var string
   */
  public $label;

}
?>
```

To provide default configuration for this type, we need to place it in a file named `cm_example.example.[bundle name].yml` and define a schema for the type in `cm_example.schema.yml`.

Let's assume that the type requires a label and a message only, and is translatable:

```
cm_example.cm_example.*:
  type: config_entity
  label: 'Example settings'
  mapping:
    id:
      type: string
      label: 'Internal Example ID'
    label:
      type: string
      label: 'Human readable label'
    message:
      type: string
      label: 'Message to display'
    langcode:
      type: string
      label: 'Default language'
```

This defines the basic structure for all bundles of the `CM Example` configuration type, as we learned in *Chapter 5*, *The Anatomy of Schema Files*.

If we now add the default configuration for this configuration entity type, we can simply create a file named `cm_example.cm_example.test.yml` and add the following code to the file:

```
# Machine-readable name.
id: test
# Define the label.
label: 'Example bundle'
# A basic message.
message: 'Configuration Management in Drupal 8'
# Default language.
langcode: 'en'
```

During the installation of our module, Drupal will then create an entity named `test` of the type `CM Example` based on the values defined in the default configuration file (assuming we have already implemented the corresponding functions to save the entities of our configuration type).

Using the configuration

We already learned how to use the Configuration Management API to access configuration objects in the previous chapters. The simplest way to use your configuration is the `\Drupal::config()` method and `\Drupal::configFactory()->getEditable()`:

```php
<?php
// Load all settings from 'cm_example.settings.yml'.
$settings = \Drupal::config('cm_example.settings');
// Get number of items per page.
$items_per_page = $settings->get('items_per_page');
?>
```

This will load the current value of the simple configuration `items_per_page`. If the value hasn't been changed by a user or overridden by another module, the variable will hold the default value provided by our module.

As described before, you can also modify the configuration:

```php
<?php
// Change items per page and save to active configuration.
\Drupal::configFactory()->getEditable('cm_example.settings')-
  >set('items_per_page', '10')->save();
?>
```

Now that we have equipped our example module with some default configuration, and added our own configuration entity type, we would like some users to change the basic settings of our module.

Creating a configuration form

Now that we know how to add custom configuration to our module and how to provide some configuration defaults, we will learn how to enable certain users to change the configuration values in the user interface. To do this, we need to create a custom form for our configuration values and define a path on which the form will be accessible.

Configuration forms in Drupal 7

First, let's take a look back at Drupal 7. In Drupal 7, we needed to add an implementation of `hook_menu()` to our custom module to tell Drupal from which path users might access our configuration form:

```php
<?php
/**
 * Implements hook_menu().
 */
function cm_example_menu() {
  $items = array();

  // Define path to configuration page.
  $items['admin/config/example'] = array(
    'title' => 'Example configuration',
    'description' => 'Configure settings for Example.',
    'page callback' => 'drupal_get_form',
    'page arguments' => array('cm_example_settings_form'),
    'access arguments' => array('access administration pages'),
  );

  return $items;
}
?>
```

This will register the path `admin/config/example` to our page built in Drupal 7, and ensure that the specified function to generate our configuration page will be called. To simplify things a bit, we use `drupal_get_form()` as the page callback function here and hand over the name of our form generation function as an argument to it. The `cm_example_settings_form()` function itself wasn't very complicated. You define your form elements and return the form structure wrapped by `system_settings_form()`. This function includes the necessary elements (that is, the submit button), adds the required validation, and submits callbacks to the form, so you don't need to bother about saving the values. It maps the form's fields to variables using the variable system:

```php
<?php
/**
 * Form generation callback for Example settings in Drupal 7.
 */
function cm_example_settings_form() {
  $form = array();

  $form['items_per_page'] = array(
```

```
      '#type' => 'textfield',
      '#title' => t('Items per page'),
      '#description' => t('The number of Example items per page.'),
      '#default_value' => variable_get('items_per_page', 10),
    );
    // Return the wrapped form structure.
    return system_settings_form($form);
  }
?>
```

In real life, you would prefix the settings name with the name of your module to avoid naming collisions with other modules or Drupal itself. In our example, this would create a simple form with a single text field and would save the entered value without any further validation to the variables table.

Creating configuration forms in Drupal 8

In Drupal 8, things have changed a lot when it comes to form building. As shown in the previous pages, in Drupal 7, you simply add a menu hook definition and a form creation function that returns a renderable array. Since Drupal 8 uses object-oriented programming, forms are defined using classes.

So, to create a configuration form for our configuration, we need to:

- Add a form controller class that is responsible for creating the form elements and handles validation and submission
- Add a route to define a path for the form
- Add a menu item for the form

Adding a form controller

At first, we need to create a form controller that is responsible for form generation and handles additional validation and saving of the submitted values. Since we do not want to build the controller from scratch, we simply extend the existing `ConfigFormBase` class. This class is Drupal 8's replacement for `system_settings_form()`, familiar from Drupal 7 and before.

The form controller class is saved to a file named `ExampleSettingsForm.php`. Since we would like to keep our code organized, we put this file in the `src\Form` subdirectory of our module. To create the basic class, we need to define the namespace of the class and override the `getFormId()` and `getEditableConfigNames()` functions of the basic `FormInterface` interface. The returned string identifies the form across the system and must be unique for your site. It is a best practice to use the name of the defining module as a prefix again, so we simply use `cm_example_settings_form` as the identifier in our example:

```php
<?php
/**
 * @file
 * Contains \Drupal\cm_example\Form\ExampleSettingsForm.
 */

namespace Drupal\cm_example\Form;

use Drupal\Core\Form\ConfigFormBase;
use Drupal\Core\Form\FormStateInterface;

/**
 * Provides the site configuration form.
 */
class ExampleSettingsForm extends ConfigFormBase {

  /**
   * {@inheritdoc}
   */
  public function getFormId() {
    return 'cm_example_settings_form';
    }

  /**
   * {@inheritdoc}
   */
  protected function getEditableConfigNames() {
    return ['cm_example.settings'];
  }
}
?>
```

The `getEditableConfigNames()` function returns the names of configuration items that the form should be able to edit. Drupal then automatically uses the correct getter for your configuration if you access the values through `$this->config()`. If the configuration object is requested as editable, a call to `\Drupal::configFactory()->getEditable()` is made internally; otherwise, it is simply `\Drupal::config()->get()`.

Now, we create the needed form elements for our configuration by overriding the `buildForm()` function:

```php
<?php
  /**
   * {@inheritdoc}
   */
  public function buildForm(array $form, FormStateInterface $form_
state) {
    $config = $this->config('cm_example.settings');

    $form['example'] = array(
      '#type' => 'fieldgroup',
      '#title' => $this->t('Example'),
    );
    $form['example']['items_per_page'] = array(
      '#type' => 'textfield',
      '#title' => $this->t('Items per page'),
      '#default_value' => $config->get('items_per_page'),
      '#required' => TRUE,
      '#weight' => -20,
    );

    return parent::buildForm($form, $form_state);
  }
?>
```

As you can see, this is not very different from the function used in Drupal 7. The only major differences are the use of the `ConfigFactory` class (available through `$this->config()`) and the call to the parent class's `buildForm()` function.

The last missing piece for the form controller class is a submission handler. Unlike using Drupal 7's `system_settings_form()`, we need to manually save the submitted configuration values:

```php
<?php
  /**
   * {@inheritdoc}
```

```
  */
  public function submitForm(array &$form, FormStateInterface $form_
state) {
    $this->config('cm_example.settings')
          ->set('items_per_page', $form_state->getValue('items_per_
page'))
          ->save();

    parent::submitForm($form, $form_state);
  }
?>
```

Route and menu items

Making a page accessible on your site is not as easy as it has been in former Drupal versions. Instead of adding the path using `hook_menu()`, you need to define a so-called route.

The route is defined in a file called `cm_example.routing.yml` and placed in the root directory of our module:

```
cm_example.settings:
  path: '/admin/config/cm_example/settings'
  defaults:
    _form: '\Drupal\cm_example\Form\ExampleSettingsForm'
    _title: 'Example settings'
  requirements:
    _permission: 'administer site configuration'
```

In the `cm_example.routing.yml` file, we define the path from which the configuration form will be accessible, and map the form we created using the Form Controller. Additionally, we define the page title and set some permission (so that unprivileged users cannot change these settings).

Even though we defined the route here, we still need to manually add an item to the menu so that the site's user can simply access the page without manually entering the path every time.

For the new menu item, we would like to create a new group on `admin/config` to visually separate the item from other pages. To create such a group, we need to edit `cm_example.routing.yml` again and add the following lines:

```
cm_example.admin_config_cmexample:
  path: '/admin/config/cm_example'
  defaults:
```

```
    _controller: '\Drupal\system\Controller\SystemController::systemAd
minMenuBlockPage'
    _title: 'CM Example'
  requirements:
    _permission: 'access administration pages'
```

As you can see, we use the core function `systemAdminMenuBlockPage()` of the `SystemController` class here, so we don't need to implement any other classes.

To add the menu item to this group, we now create a file named `cm_example.links.menu.yml` in the root folder of our module as follows:

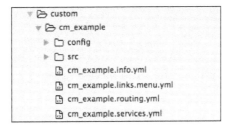

Within this file, we define a menu item for the previously created group (an automatically created overview page such as `admin/config/system`), and define the menu item for our custom settings form that we created earlier in this chapter:

```
cm_example.admin_config_cmexample:
  title: 'CM Example'
  route_name: cm_example.admin_config_cmexample
  parent: system.admin_config
  description: 'CM Example settings.'
  weight: 0
cm_example.example_settings:
  title: 'CM Example settings'
  parent: cm_example.admin_config_cmexample
  description: 'Change settings of CM Example.'
  route_name: cm_example.settings
  weight: 0
```

For a menu item, we add the name of the corresponding route (the `route_name` key) that defines the path to follow, and a parent for the item. The value of the `parent` key is the key of the menu item that you want your item to be a child of; thus, to put our overview page below `admin/config`, we need to set `system.admin_config` as the parent here.

The result

Visiting `admin/config` after installing the example module will now give you a new group that contains a link to the configuration form as follows:

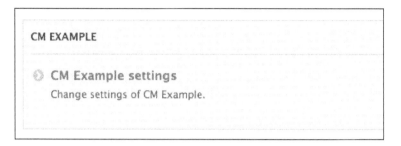

Calling `admin/config/cm_example` gives you the automatically created overview page of all menu items that have the `cm_example.admin_config_cmexample` route:

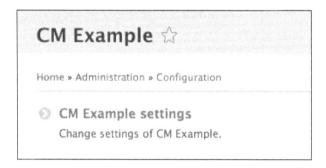

Finally, clicking on the link will direct us to our settings form in all its beauty, as shown in the following screenshot:

Summary

As you can see, it is not very complicated to add a default configuration to your Drupal 8 module and to create a custom form for your configuration.

Drupal 8 provides you with powerful tools to define the form and create the required menu items, so you can focus on the form itself and give your users a good user experience.

Having to upgrade a configuration defined in previous versions, though, is not as simple. In the next chapter, we will describe how to upgrade your variables from older versions of Drupal to make them available with the new Configuration Management system.

7
Upgrading Your Drupal 7 Variables to the Drupal 8 Configuration

In the previous chapters, we prepared you to add configuration data and schema files to your Drupal 8 modules. But what about all the old modules written for Drupal 7? How do you convert the variables introduced there to new configuration objects? And how can we convert the old setting forms to the forms used by the Configuration System in Drupal 8?

This chapter will show you some ways to convert your Drupal 7 variables to the Drupal 8 Configuration objects and how to provide an upgrade path in your modules.

Upgrading your variables

When upgrading your variables from Drupal 7 to Drupal 8, you first need to identify whether the variables are a simple configuration (for example, the number of nodes displayed to a user) or whether you need to create a more complex configuration object (for example, an image style). Some variables, though, are not meant to be permanent (for example, the time of the last Cron run); additionally, therefore, you will have to decide if it should be a configuration (which is permanent by definition) or a state (which reflects information about the current site's state, but we will come back to this later).

Simple configuration

Let's start with a simple example and a simple variable to convert. Simple variables are, for example, the number of nodes on the front page, the name of your site, or whether your site is in maintenance mode.

We assume that our module built for Drupal 7 uses variables to store settings that a user might configure. So, the module provides a small form to save the settings:

```php
<?php
/**
 * Page callback for Drupal 7 example settings form.
 */
function cm_example_settings($form, &$form_state) {
  // Saved/default value of variable "items_per_page".
  $items_per_page = variable_get('cm_example_items_per_page', 20);
  // Create the corresponding form element.
  $form['items_per_page'] = array(
    '#type' => 'textfield',
    '#title' => t('Items per page'),
    '#description' => t('Enter the number of items per page.'),
    '#default_value' => $items_per_page,
    '#element_validate' => array('element_validate_integer'),
  );

  // Saved/default value of variable "header".
  $header = variable_get('cm_example_header', TRUE);
  $form['header'] = array(
    '#type' => 'checkbox',
    '#title' => t('Display list header'),
    '#default_value' => $header,
  );

  // Create form actions.
  $form['actions'] = array(
    ['#type'] = 'actions',
  );
  $form['actions']['submit'] = array(
    '#type' => 'submit',
    '#value' => t('Save configuration'),
  );

  // Return the form structure to pass to drupal_get_form().
```

```
    return $form;
  }
  ?>
```

Normally, we would use `system_settings_form()` to add the submit button and the submit callback. However, since we would like to display the use of `variable_set()`, we manually save our variables, as shown in the following code:

```php
<?php
/**
 * Submit callback for Drupal 7 example settings.
 */
function cm_example_settings_submit($form, &$form_state) {
  // Save the variables (preprend the variable names with the
  // module name to prevent naming conflicts).
  $items_per_page = $form_state['values']['items_per_page'];
  variable_set('cm_example_items_per_page', $items_per_page);
  $header = $form_state['values']['header'];
  variable_set('cm_example_header', $header);

  drupal_set_message('The configuration options have been saved.');
}
?>
```

As the variables shown in our example code are all simple items, we can easily convert them to a simple configuration in Drupal 8. All of these settings can be stored in a configuration object named `<module_name>.settings`.

We've already learned how to put simple settings provided by a module in a file named `<module_name>.settings.yml` in your module's `config/install` directory. In our example, this is `cm_example.settings.yml`:

```
# Configuration for the CM Example module.
items_per_page: 20
header: 1
```

Make sure you create a schema file too, otherwise your configuration won't be correctly recognized by Drupal:

```
# Schema for the configuration files of the CM Example module.
cm_example.settings:
  type: mapping
  label: 'CM Example settings'
  mapping:
    items_per_page:
      type: integer
```

```
    label: 'Items per page'
  header:
    type: boolean
    label: 'Display list header'
```

Now, you can easily convert all the calls made to `variable_get()` to the new `\Drupal::config($name)->get($key)` calls:

```php
<?php
// Drupal 7:
$items_per_page = variable_get('cm_example_items_per_page', 20);

// Drupal 8:
$items_per_page = \Drupal::config('cm_example.settings')->get('items_
per_page');
?>
```

Converting the calls to `variable_set()` is basically what we did for `variable_get()`; we simply replace the function calls with the setter function of `ConfigFactory`. Remember to use `\Drupal::configFactory()->getEditable()` here since you cannot change any configuration loaded with `\Drupal::config()`:

```php
<?php
// Drupal 7:
variable_set('cm_example_items_per_page', $items_per_page);

// Drupal 8:
\Drupal::configFactory->getEditable('cm_example.settings')
  ->set('items_per_page', $items_per_page)
  ->save();
?>
```

When using `\Drupal::config()` or `\Drupal::configFactory->getEditable()` multiple times for the same configuration object within one functional block, it is much better to invoke it only once:

```php
<?php
// Load mutable configuration object.
$config = \Drupal::configFactory->getEditable('cm_example.settings');
// Access single configuration value.
$items_per_page = $config->get('items_per_page');
$header = $config->get('header');

// Modify values.
$items_per_page = 10;
```

```
$header = FALSE;

// Save configuration value.
$config->set('items_per_page', $items_per_page)
  ->set('header', $header)
  ->save();
?>
```

This way, you can avoid multiple unnecessary reads of the configuration and a decrease in performance.

Complex configuration objects

If you have used more complex settings in your Drupal 7 module (such as image styles or filter formats), you could consider creating a custom Configuration Entity Type as we showed in the previous chapter. For example, image styles have been converted to Configuration Entity Types, including image effects as plugins in Drupal 8.

Assume you would like to convert an image style named news provided by your Drupal 7 module to a Drupal 8 configuration object. First, you will create a file named image.style.news.yml (according to the naming convention, <module_name>.<config_object_name>{.<optional_sub_key>}.yml). This file will hold the entire definition of your image style:

```
name: news
label: 'News (240x160)'
effects:
  148b5b70-be82-11e3-b1b6-0800200c9a66:
    id: image_scale
    data:
      width: 240
      height: 160
      upscale: true
    weight: 0
    uuid: 148b5b70-be82-11e3-b1b6-0800200c9a66
langcode: en
```

Now you scan your module's files for code that contains the image style options (for example, the width of the used effect) and replace it with calls to the corresponding load() function:

```
<?php
// Drupal 7:
// Load the image style.
```

```
if (($style = image_style_load('news')) !== FALSE) {
  // List all associated effects for this style.
  $effects = image_style_effects($style);
  // Assume the effect has ieid "1".
  $effect_width = $effects[1]['data']['width'];
}


// Drupal 8:
// Load entity of type "Image Style".
$style = entity_load('image_style', 'news');
// Get the effect definition.
$effect_scale = $style->getEffect('148b5b70-be82-11e3-b1b6-
0800200c9a66');
// Get dimensions of selected effect.
$dimensions = array(
  'height' => 0,
  'width' => 0,
);
$effect_scale->transformDimensions($dimensions);
// Get the value of property "width".
$effect_width = $dimensions['width'],
?
```

As you can see, configuration entities simplify things a lot, and the code is much easier to handle.

Upgrading to the new state system

Sometimes, you use variables in your modules that represent a state of the system. For example, if your module regularly fetches data from a different site, you may want to store the time of the last fetch; alternatively, and taking Drupal itself as an example, the time of the last cron run or maintenance mode are not persistent configuration but are specific to the current environment. This information has no use in deployment, and therefore should not be saved as configuration data.

Fortunately, the State API is very similar to the Configuration API. To get a specific value from the state system, simply use $value = \Drupal::state()->get($key);. Setting values is simply \Drupal::state()->set($key, $value);.

For example, if you would like to get maintenance mode, you would do this:

```
$mode = \Drupal::state()->get('system.maintenance_mode');
```

Providing an upgrade path for your variables

Unfortunately, providing an upgrade path for variables used in modules for Drupal 6 or Drupal 7 is not as easy as simply fetching the values from the database and storing them into the new configuration system. You need to convert the variables into configuration objects, performing the correct data conversions and saving the values correctly.

Prior to Drupal 8, upgrading between major versions of Drupal was mainly done using `hook_update_N()`. The developer used this hook to move the required data from the old data structure into the new one, and was responsible for all conversions needed for the data to work in the new version of the site. In 2013, during DrupalCon in Prague, the decision was made to disallow these old-style upgrades and use a new and much more flexible approach for this task: the **Migrate** module.

Migrating your data

The best way to securely upgrade existing variables to the new configuration system is by using Migrate (a module that has now been built into Drupal 8's core).

Migrate has been around for a couple of years as a contributed module in Drupal. It gives you near endless possibilities for migrating content into Drupal from other sources. This isn't limited to Drupal-to-Drupal conversions; you are also able to import from CMS, XML, JSON, or any other parsable source.

So, to inform Drupal about the variables that we would like to upgrade to Drupal 8, we need to define a migration configuration. The naming schema of the migration configuration files is `migrate.migration.<identifier>.yml`.

For the `cm_example` module that we used in the previous chapters, we use `d7_cm_example_settings` as the identifier because we would like to provide an upgrade path from Drupal 7 for the variables defined by our module:

```
id: d7_cm_example_settings
label: Drupal 7 CM example configuration
migration_groups:
  - CM example
source:
  plugin: variable
  variables:
    - cm_example_items_per_page
    - cm_example_header
```

```
process:
  items_per_page: cm_example_items_per_page
  header: cm_example_header
destination:
  plugin: config
  config_name: cm_example.settings
```

This tells Drupal to convert all the listed variables to the new configuration object `cm_example.settings`.

Let's dissect the previous example:

- `id`: This is the unique identifier for the migration. This is the same identifier that we used in order to create the filename.

- `label`: This is a human-readable description for the migration.

- `migration_groups`: This is a list of group names for creating bundles of migrations that can be executed together (for example, migrations converting a site from Drupal 7 to Drupal 8 or all migrations importing data from XML).

- `source`: This defines the plugin used to collect the source data and arguments used by this plugin. In our example, we use the `variable` plugin to fetch the variables named `cm_example_items_per_page` and `cm_example_header` from the database of our Drupal 7 database.

- `process`: This describes how the migrate destination is constructed from the source data. We simply map the names of our new configuration items with the old variable names, so the data that comes from the Drupal 7 variable `cm_example_header` will be mapped to the configuration item `cm_example.settings.header`.

- `destination`: This is similar to the source, but (obviously) defines the destination plugin responsible for transforming the incoming data into the desired format. Since we would like to save the old variables into a configuration object, `config` is used as the destination, and the name of our configuration object is passed as an argument to the plugin.

For more complex examples (such as complex data alterations or dependencies), just examine the `migrate.*.yml` files within the core module `Migrate Drupal`.

Source plugins

To tell Drupal which type of data you would like to upgrade, you will need to specify the source plugin for your migration:

```
source:
  plugin: variable
  variables:
    - cm_example_items_per_page
    - cm_example_header
```

Since we are upgrading our variables, we will use the `variable` source plugin here. There is a whole bunch of source plugins available, for blocks, comments, fields, and so on—just anything you need to upgrade a simple Drupal site.

To specify which variables to upgrade, simply add the `variables` subkey and list the names of the variables as they are stored in the table {`variables`} of your old site. Depending on the plugin used as the source, there are eventually other arguments you need to add. For example, the `term` source requires you to specify a vocabulary.

Process plugins

For a clean migration, Drupal needs to know how to handle the properties of your data. This is described in the `process` key of a migration configuration. The plugin used here is responsible for mapping the incoming data to the new structure:

```
process:
  items_per_page: cm_example_items_per_page
  header: cm_example_header
```

Each property to be processed during the migration is entered as a child key of `process`. The value of such a property key is either the name of the source property or an associative array. In the previous example, we need a simple 1:1 mapping, so it is safe to use the name of the new configuration item as the key and the name of the Drupal 7 variable as the value.

If the source data needs some special processing, the value is written as an associative array. It contains a `plugin` key that identifies the plugin to use for the mapping and additional values used by the specified process plugin. An example of such a process plugin is to use an author ID from a different migration:

```
process:
  uid:
    plugin: migration
    migration: users
    source: author
```

This tells Drupal to use the value of the property `author`, which has been defined in a migration named `users` as the data source of the new property `uid`.

It is even possible to pass the source value through multiple plugins to get the correct structure and value for the destination property. To do this, you need to add a list of plugin configurations to the destination key.

The Drupal 6 migration for filter formats, for example, passes the name of the old format to a process plugin to create a machine name, and then reduces potential duplicated values:

```
process:
  format:
    -
      plugin: machine_name
      source: name
    -
      plugin: dedupe_entity
      entity_type: filter_format
      field: format
      length: 32
```

If you are using a nested data structure (for example, if the source is `$source['defaults']['page']['items_per_page']`), you need to use `'defaults/page/items_per_page'` as the value (or as the key when setting the value to a nested configuration object).

Some examples of process plugins are:

- `get`: This is the simplest process plugin and simply maps the data exactly from the source to the destination. You do not even need to specify the plugin but can simply use the shorthand notation:

```
process:
  items_per_page: cm_example_items_per_page
```

- callback: This is used to process the source value using custom or built-in functions:

```
process:
  destination:
    plugin: callback
    callable: strtolower
  source: source_field
```

It is even possible to use a method within a specific class. In this case, you need to identify the names of the class and the function as an array for the key callable:

```
process:
  plugin: callback
    callable:
    - '\Drupal\Component\Utility\Unicode'
    - strtolower
  source: source_field
```

- default_value: This simply sets a default value for a destination property. This plugin is useful in combination with other plugins, so you can add a default value if other plugins in the process pipeline fail to fetch a value:

```
process:
  uid:
    -

      plugin: migration
      id: users
      source: author

    -

      plugin: default_value
      default_value: 1
```

For a complete list of process plugins provided by the Drupal core, visit the Migrate handbook at https://www.drupal.org/node/2129651.

Destination plugins

After defining the data source and how to process each property in it, we need to tell Drupal where to put the processed data. This is done with destination plugins. For entities, the value of the plugin key typically is entity:{entity_type}. For example:

```
destination:
  plugin: entity:block
```

For our purpose, we will use the `config` plugin that gives us the ability to save the processed data into configuration objects.

The plugin simply accepts the name of a configuration object:

```
destination:
  plugin: config
  config_name: cm_example.settings
```

Since Drupal can handle only one destination per migration, you need to create multiple migrations if you need to split your old variables into different configuration objects.

Drupal 8 provides several predefined destination plugins (such as comments, files, or taxonomy terms), so usually you don't need to create your own for a simple site.

Running the migration

At the time of writing, running the migration is not that easy. Unfortunately, there is no user interface in the Drupal core to execute a migration, so you will need to use Drush (version 7.x and above). Some work has been done on a user interface for Migrate (https://www.drupal.org/project/migrate_upgrade), but it is still unclear when and if this will be moved into Drupal 8's core.

To migrate data from one site to another, Drupal needs to know which migrations should be executed. This needs to be defined in a so-called manifest file. The following are the conditions that the manifest file should fulfill:

- It must be saved directly in Drupal's root directory
- It must be a simple text file
- It obviously needs to list all migrations you wish to execute (including their dependencies)

The name of the manifest file doesn't matter, but it should be named something similar to `manifest.yml` (even if it is a simple text file, we should use the `.yml` extension to create some kind of convention).

Here is a short example on how such a manifest could look:

```
# Example for Drupal 7 to Drupal 8 migration
d7_cm_example_settings
d7_cm_example_block
d7_block
d7_filter_format
```

You do not need to bother about the order of the listed migrations within your manifest since Migrate will automatically reorder them based on the individual dependencies each migration has.

Finally, to run the migrations, we need to execute the Drush command `migrate-manifest`:

```
drush migrate-manifest <path/to/manifest> --legacy-db-url=<database-
connection-string>
```

Summary

Updating your modules to use the new configuration objects instead of variables is really easy and makes your code much more readable and flexible. After reading this chapter, you should now be able to differentiate between persistent configuration (deployable) using the Configuration API and environment-specific data using the State API.

Upgrading a Drupal 6 site to Drupal 7 seems easier at first glance since you simply have to run `update.php` after preparing the site and updating the code base. However, as soon as you have installed some contrib modules, it gets complicated. The modules need to convert their data to the correct structure, and sometimes, you need to write your own update hooks. Using Migrate as the base tool for major version upgrades is much more flexible and robust.

In the next chapter, we will show you how to deal with configuration on multilingual sites and how you can provide translations for configuration.

8
Managing Configuration for Multilingual Websites

Drupal allows you to build comprehensive multilingual websites in which you can display content in different languages and translate the user interface.

While many features had been built into the Drupal core in previous versions, building multilingual sites was a very painful task.

In this chapter, we will take a look at how Drupal 7 deals with different languages on a site and how Drupal 8 is trying to fix the weaknesses from the previous versions.

Multilingual sites in Drupal 7

In Drupal 7, it wasn't very easy to create multilingual sites and make all your content and settings translatable. There were too many components that utilized different ways to translate content, and all of these components had too many dependencies. Even for experienced site builders, it could be a real struggle to set up those components and dependencies.

We will describe some of the basic aspects of Drupal 7's multilingual approach before covering details of multilingual sites in Drupal 8.

The Locale module

The main translation component in Drupal 7 was the *Locale* module. It gives you basic language support and is responsible for translating the site's user interface. Without the Locale module, you cannot set up your site to display texts in another language, and you will also be unable to translate common strings, such as the text on submit buttons.

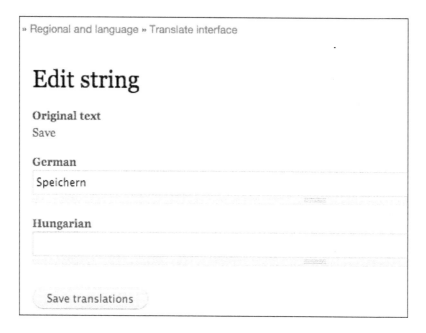

As shown in the preceding image, the Locale module makes it very easy to translate strings on your site as long as they are provided using the t() function (see https://api.drupal.org/api/search/7/t).

To avoid translating all the strings manually, you can install the Localization update module, which downloads translations for Drupal itself and for contributed modules on installation. Additionally, it updates translations for you after a module has been updated, and makes sure the translation matches the current installed version. The translations for Drupal's core and many contributed modules are created by the community and are available on https://localize.drupal.org. By default, Localization update fetches its data from this official server, but you can also create your own translation source and let Localization update get the translations from your custom server.

Content translation

Having a multilingual user interface and being able to translate the interface text used on the site isn't enough for most sites. Most users would like to have their content available in different languages too. For example, some news items only apply to visitors located in English-speaking countries, while other items are of interest for people in Hungary.

So, in Drupal 7, you needed to install the Content translation module that comes with Drupal 7 by default so you didn't need to download it separately.

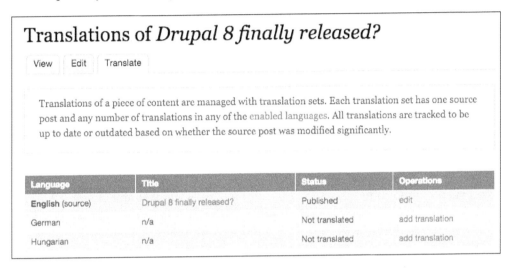

This module gives you the ability to translate single nodes into different languages. For every translation, it creates a copy of the translated node, so you will have one node per language.

The main drawback of this module is that it can be used only for nodes, and does not handle translation of other types of content.

Translating other types of content

To translate other types of content—such as taxonomy terms, views, menus and menu items, or field labels—you need at least one other additional module, Internationalization (i18n). This is the base module for the translation of entities other than nodes. To make things just a little more complex, there are some more modules required to enable translation of this type of content, such as Internationalization Views (i18n_views), Webform Localization (webform_ localization), and many more. Unfortunately, there has been no real standard on how to implement translatability, so nearly every module that defines its own type of content needs a different module for translation, and you'll end up installing more and more modules to translate your content.

Translation settings/configuration

As you might guess, there is still something missing when translating your Drupal 7 site—that is, the configuration defined by Drupal itself and the contributed modules you have installed on the site. Think of your site's slogan, the site name, or the e-mails sent to users after registration. You surely want to deliver these in the language that the user prefers.

So you need another bundle of modules—for example, *Variable* and *Variable translation* (part of the *Internalization* module). After installing those, you are able to translate variables too, but only if the module that defines the variable provides integration for the *Variable* module.

Site information

There are *multilingual* variables in this form

Check you are editing the variables for the right Language value or select the desired Language.

English | **German** | Hungarian

Site details

Site name *

Konfigurationsmanagement in Drupal 7

This is a multilingual variable.

Slogan

How this is used depends on your site's theme. **This is a multilingual variable.**

So, every form that handles multilingual variables is modified to provide translation capabilities for these variables. Sometimes, the translation form does not show all the variables of the original form because not all variables are translatable. This can be very confusing at times.

Translating entities

Finally, even after translating all the other stuff, custom entities are still missing. Have you ever heard of *Drupal Commerce* (you need this if you are building a shop on your site) or *Bean* (a replacement for the block system in Drupal 7)? If you need to make these entities translatable (and of course, others too), you need to install *Entity translation* and some other modules.

So, to sum it up, you easily need to install 30+ modules to create a fully multilingual site in Drupal 7 and configure all those modules correctly. This is a real struggle and could take a lot of time.

Not to forget the poor content editors and site administrators who have to find the correct pages to translate the stuff. Every type of translation has a different user interface located on a different path with a different set of permissions, so translating your site isn't really much fun.

Translating in Drupal 8

Drupal 8 wouldn't be Drupal 8 if it didn't change translation as it changes everything else. The Drupal 8 Multilingual Initiative, under the lead of Gábor Hojtsy, did a great job and reworked nearly everything that was related to translation.

In Drupal 8, there are 4 main pillars for translation:

- **Language**: This is the base service for all modules that deal with data on your site. Even if you don't actually use translation features, it manages languages wherever you may need them on your site or within your modules. Additionally, it is responsible for language detection and selecting the correct language in which to deliver your translated content and configuration.

- **Interface**: The interface component supports translation of Drupal itself, as it provides all the tools to translate the interface strings (as they were known in previous versions).

- **Content**: In contrast to Drupal 7's *Content translation* module, this handles the translation of all fields for all defined entities on a site (similar to *Entity translation* in Drupal 7). It isn't limited to nodes, but will manage the translation of all other entity types too.

- **Configuration**: Every configuration defined as translatable is translated using this component. It makes sure you can translate simple configuration—for example, the site's name, its slogan, or complex configuration such as blocks, views, or field settings (for instance labels).

Configuration translation

As mentioned before, every configuration, whether provided by Drupal itself or a contributed module, can be translated if it's defined as translatable and after you enable the core module *Configuration translation*. The language of the configuration (either a simple configuration or a complex configuration) is tracked directly in the responsible configuration object. We expand `cm_example.settings.yml` with 2 more keys, `description` and `langcode`, as follows:

```
items_per_page: 20
header: 1
description: ''
langcode: en
```

The `langcode` key you see in the previous example defines the default language for translatable items within this configuration object.

To enable translation for a configuration item, you need to add a flag to the corresponding schema to tell Drupal that this configuration item can be translatable:

```
# Schema for the configuration files of the CM Example module.

cm_example.settings:
  type: mapping
  label: 'CM Example settings'
  mapping:
    description:
      type: string
      label: 'Item description'
      translatable: true
```

Even a data type can identify itself as translatable. When creating a custom configuration data type, you can also add the `translatable` property; all the configuration items using this type will then be translatable by default, without your having to specify them individually. For example, the `date_format` core data type does this, and also defines a translation context:

```
# PHP Date format string that is translatable.
date_format:
  type: string
```

```
label: 'Date format'
translatable: true
translation context: 'PHP date format'
```

Translating the configuration

After installing the *Configuration translation* module, you will get a **Translate...** tab on the configuration page of your module (and on all other pages that show configuration forms), as shown in the following screenshot:

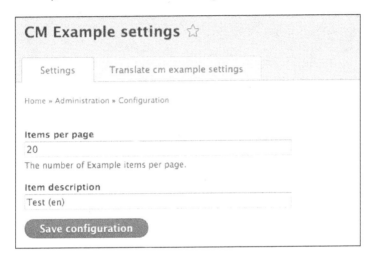

Clicking on the link will route you to a listing of all possible languages this configuration can be translated to, as shown in the following screenshot:

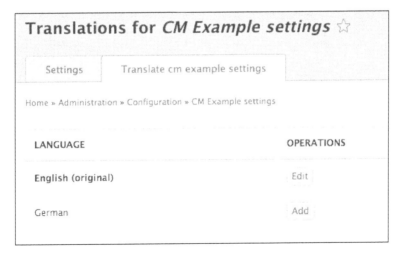

You can either edit the item in the original language, which will bring you back to the default configuration form, or add a translation for the configuration items. On the translation page, you will see only the items marked as translatable in the following schema (as shown in the previous example):

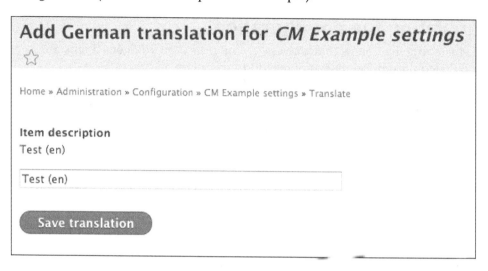

Of course, translation also applies to other configuration objects. If you would like to translate the title of a block, you simply go to its configuration page and click on the **Translate block** tab. Now, you can see the language listing we talked about earlier and can translate the block, as shown in the following screenshot:

To get an overview of all available translatable configuration, Drupal provides a listing of all these items at `admin/config/regional/config-translation`, as shown in the following screenshot:

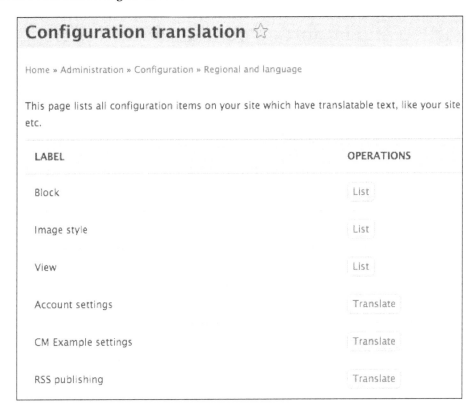

As you can see, there are two different types listed: simple configuration objects (such as **Account settings**) that can be translated directly, and sets of entities, where you are directed to a list of items of that type (such as **Image style**).

Storing translations

The translation is also stored as configuration, using the same storage mechanism as a normal configuration, so it is treated just like the configuration itself. The name of the translated configuration object equates to the original object, but is associated with a different so-called `collection`.

For translations, the schema for a collection name is usually `language.{language-code}` — for example `language.de` for a German translation.

Translating our configuration object defined in `cm_example.settings` in to German would result in an entry named `cm_example.settings` in the database, with the collection set to `language.de`.

Exporting and importing configuration translations

Manual translation of your site's configuration isn't the only way to create a completely multilingual site. You can also import existing translations into your current site, so you don't have to do all the editing by hand.

At the time of writing, the only way to export configuration translations is to do a full export of your site's configuration.

Doing a full export of the site's configuration would create a directory named `language` within the export. For each language translated, a configuration value would be created in another subdirectory within `language`. These language-specific directories contain files for all translated configuration objects, as shown in the following screenshot:

In our case, the `cm_example.settings.yml` file would only contain the `description` key, since this is the only translatable configuration value set up for translation:

```
description: Test (de)
```

Assume you've translated the configuration in your development environment and would like to make the translation available on the live site. First, you will need to export the current translation (by doing a full export on `admin/config/development/configuration/full/export`).

On the target website, you can then simply import the translation by copying the `language` directory with all its files from the exported archive to the staging directory of the target website. Note that this directory needs to contain all configuration files you've exported, since any configuration missing here will be deleted from the active storage on the target site during the import.

There, you will need to navigate to `admin/config/development/configuration` to view the configuration changes:

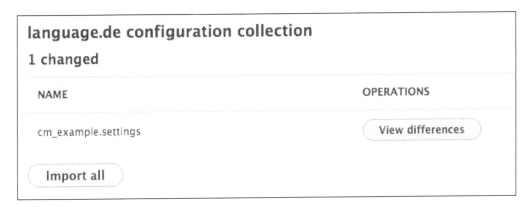

You can even view the differences between the active configuration and the new values before importing, so you don't end up with unwanted an configuration or translation.

It is also possible to ship a default configuration translation with your own module. To do this, you simply need to create a directory structure such as the one described before within the `config/install` directory of your module, and put the `.yml` files with your translated configuration values in it:

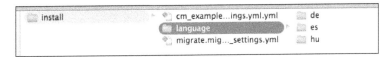

Note that shipping the translation with your module shouldn't be done if you host your project at `https://drupal.org` because in that case, the translation is created by the community (or yourself) and hosted at `https://localize.drupal.org`. Additionally, the Interface translation module downloads and manages translations of modules hosted at `https://drupal.org` or on a custom localization server you registered to use.

Summary

In this chapter, we've seen that it was difficult to build a multilingual site in Drupal 7. You had to install various modules and implement many different settings to allow your users to translate every type of content and configuration on the site.

In Drupal 8, this process has been rebuilt completely, so you can make your site multilingual with just a few clicks and give your users simple tools to translate the missing pieces.

Now that you have learned so much about the different types of configuration, how to upgrade your configuration from previous versions of Drupal, and how to make the configuration translatable, we will show you some tools and resources you might want to try out in the next chapter.

Useful Tools and Getting Help

9

When dealing with Configuration Management, you might get to a point where you need help. This chapter provides a list of useful links and tools provided by the Drupal community.

Your starting point should be the documentation pages on Drupal.org. These pages are maintained by members of the Drupal community, and anyone with a Drupal. org user account can add or change them.

Community documentation

The Drupal.org community documentation contains a section on Configuration Management for developers: *Configuration API in Drupal 8*, which can be found at `https://drupal.org/developing/api/8/configuration`.

This section contains several subpages with in-depth information, and is a must-read for developers who work with the Configuration Management API.

The administration guide documentation

The Drupal.org administration guide provides information about the daily or ongoing operation of a Drupal site. Configuration Management is documented in general terms in the *Managing configuration in Drupal 8* post at `https://drupal.org/documentation/administer/config`.

Contributed modules

There are a couple of contributed modules which help you developing configuration.

The configuration inspector for Drupal 8

The configuration inspector uses Drupal 8's core built-in configuration system as well as a schema system to let you inspect configuration values and the use of schemas on top of them. This makes it possible to have a developer-focused overview of all your configuration values, and perform various testing and verification tasks on your configuration schemas. The following is a screenshot taken from `https://drupal.org/project/config_inspector` this module lists the available configuration data for user.settings:

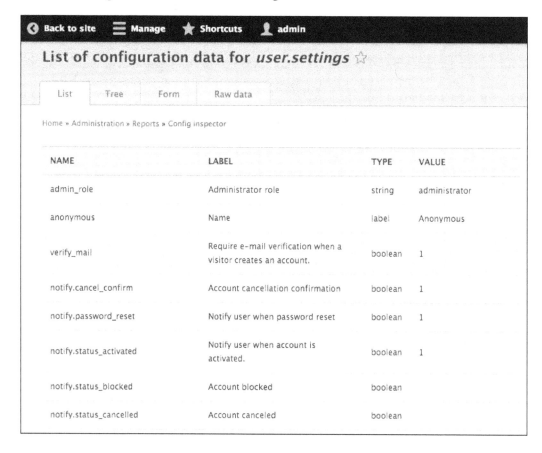

NAME	LABEL	TYPE	VALUE
admin_role	Administrator role	string	administrator
anonymous	Name	label	Anonymous
verify_mail	Require e-mail verification when a visitor creates an account.	boolean	1
notify.cancel_confirm	Account cancellation confirmation	boolean	1
notify.password_reset	Notify user when password reset	boolean	1
notify.status_activated	Notify user when account is activated.	boolean	1
notify.status_blocked	Account blocked	boolean	
notify.status_cancelled	Account canceled	boolean	

Configuration development

This module helps in developing configuration. It does the following three things:

- Importing configuration files automatically into active storage
- Exporting configuration objects automatically into files
- Helping to create modules that behave somewhat similarly to feature exporting in Drupal 7

Check the module's project page at `https://www.drupal.org/project/config_devel` for more details.

Drush

Drush is a command-line shell and scripting interface that makes life easier for people who develop websites with Drupal. If you don't know Drush yet, go visit its GitHub page at `https://github.com/drush-ops/drush`.

The tool provides some useful commands for Configuration Management.

Exporting and importing your configuration using Drush commands

The following Drush commands will be the most used ones as they allow you to export and import your configuration with a simple command:

- `drush config-export staging`: This will export the configuration from the active directory
- `drush config-import staging`: This will import the configuration from a `config` directory named `staging`

There are other commands available. We will only list the commands here. Read Drush's help documentation to find out how to use these commands, since they may have specific arguments and options. The commands are listed as follows:

- `config-get`: This will display a `config` value or a whole configuration object.
- `config-set`: This will set the `config` value directly in the active configuration.
- `config-list`: This will list config names by a prefix.
- `config-edit`: This will open a config file in a text editor. Edits are imported into the active configuration after closing the editor.

Here is an example of how to use Drush's help guide to receive more information about a command:

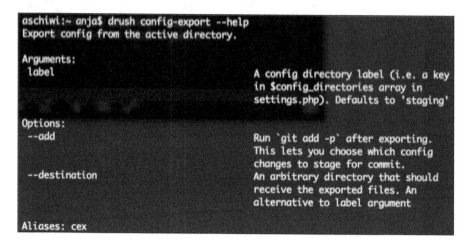

Forums

For support questions, you can visit the forum at `https://drupal.org/forum`. Make sure you do a search first because there is a very good chance that your specific question has already been answered.

The issue queue

The issue queue is where all discussions happen. It contains a vast history of the configuration system so, if you want to dig deeper, this is the place to go. You get to this issue queue by visiting Drupal's project page at `http://drupal.org/project/drupal`, and clicking through to the issues linked in the right sidebar. You should then filter by Version (8.x issues) and Component (a configuration system or configuration entity system). Here's a direct link to the configuration system queue: `https://www.drupal.org/project/issues/drupal?version=8.x&component=configuration+system`.

The direct link to the configuration entity system's issue queue is `https://www.drupal.org/project/issues/drupal?version=8.x&component=configuration+entity+system`.

The issue queue is also the place to provide patches, but you shouldn't ask for support there.

IRC chat

The Drupal community uses IRC to chat about different topics. To find out more about IRC, visit `https://drupal.org/irc`. The IRC channel for Configuration Management is `#drupal-cmi`.

Summary

Now you know some tools and how to get help, along with everything there is to know about Drupal 8's Configuration Management. Make sure you use it in your next project! Don't forget, it's important to be able to track configuration changes to your site, as it will save you time in the long run.

Do you have any questions or corrections?

Questions

You can contact us at `http://drupal-8-configuration-management.undpaul.com` if you are facing a problem with any aspect of this book, and we will do our best to address it.

Index

A

active configuration storage
  modifying 35-37
active directory
  about 30, 37
  storage location, modifying 37, 38
  versus staging directory 35
administration guide documentation
  about 119
  URL 119

C

community documentation
  URL 119
complex configuration objects 97, 98
components 8
config directory 29, 30
config files 32
configuration
  about 2
  clone, creating of site 20
  Configuration Management interface 21
  defining 79
  managing 19, 20
  single import/export 26, 27
  using 79, 83
configuration API
  about 41
  configuration data, defining 41, 42
  configuration entity types, creating 58-60
  configuration, overriding 50
  notification, obtaining for configuration
      changes 47-49

configuration changes
  tracking 3
  tracking, version control used 15, 16
configuration data
  best practices 46
  configuration object, retrieving 42, 43
  configuration values, obtaining 43, 44
  configuration values, removing 45
  configuration values, setting 44, 45
  working with 41, 42
configuration, deploying between servers
  reference link 15
configuration development
  about 121
  URL 121
configuration, Drupal 8
  global overrides 50-52
  language overrides 52-54
  module overrides 54-56
  overrides, avoiding 57, 58
  overriding 50
configuration entities
  about 16, 39
  versus simple configuration 39
configuration entity types
  basics, adding 58-60
  creating 58
  data, controlling 61
configuration file
  setting 79, 80
configuration form
  creating 83
configuration forms, Drupal 7 84, 85

S

schema files
  about 34, 63, 64
  properties 65, 66
  structure 64, 65
settings.php file
  configuration variables, storing in 13, 14
simple configuration
  about 16, 39
  example 30, 31
  versus configuration entities 39
single import/export 26, 27
source plugins 101
staging directory
  about 30, 37
  storage location, modifying 37, 38
  versus active directory 35
storage location
  modifying of active directory 37, 38
  modifying of staging directory 37, 38
sub-key references 71

T

translation, Drupal 8
  about 111
  Configuration 112
  Configuration translation 112
  Content 111
  Interface 111
  Language 111

U

upgrade path
  providing, for variables 99

V

variables
  about 12
  complex configuration objects 97, 98
  configuration 94-97
  data, migrating 99, 100
  upgrading 93
  upgrading, to new state system 98
version control
  used, for tracking configuration
    changes 15, 16
version control, best practices
  about 4
  meaningful branches 6
  meaningful commit messages 5
  work tasks, putting in project management
    tool 1
views 12

Y

YAML
  about 31
  URL 31

Thank you for buying
Drupal 8 Configuration Management

About Packt Publishing

Packt, pronounced 'packed', published its first book, *Mastering phpMyAdmin for Effective MySQL Management*, in April 2004, and subsequently continued to specialize in publishing highly focused books on specific technologies and solutions.

Our books and publications share the experiences of your fellow IT professionals in adapting and customizing today's systems, applications, and frameworks. Our solution-based books give you the knowledge and power to customize the software and technologies you're using to get the job done. Packt books are more specific and less general than the IT books you have seen in the past. Our unique business model allows us to bring you more focused information, giving you more of what you need to know, and less of what you don't.

Packt is a modern yet unique publishing company that focuses on producing quality, cutting-edge books for communities of developers, administrators, and newbies alike. For more information, please visit our website at www.packtpub.com.

About Packt Open Source

In 2010, Packt launched two new brands, Packt Open Source and Packt Enterprise, in order to continue its focus on specialization. This book is part of the Packt Open Source brand, home to books published on software built around open source licenses, and offering information to anybody from advanced developers to budding web designers. The Open Source brand also runs Packt's Open Source Royalty Scheme, by which Packt gives a royalty to each open source project about whose software a book is sold.

Writing for Packt

We welcome all inquiries from people who are interested in authoring. Book proposals should be sent to author@packtpub.com. If your book idea is still at an early stage and you would like to discuss it first before writing a formal book proposal, then please contact us; one of our commissioning editors will get in touch with you.

We're not just looking for published authors; if you have strong technical skills but no writing experience, our experienced editors can help you develop a writing career, or simply get some additional reward for your expertise.

Building a Website with Drupal
Irene Kraus

Building a Website with Drupal [Video]

ISBN: 978-1-78216-614-6   Duration: 02:27 hours

Get hands-on expertise with this comprehensive tutorial on Drupal

1. Watch how a community-oriented website including a forum and blog is built using a test server through actual deployment.

2. Learn how to add fields to existing content types and how to create new ones to match the requirements for a site.

3. Explore views and more to enhance your site and learn how to build page templates without writing any PHP code.

Drupal 7
Create and operate any type of website quickly and efficiently

David Mercer

Drupal 7

ISBN: 978-1-84951-286-2   Paperback: 416 pages

Create and operate any type of website quickly and efficiently

1. Set up, configure, and deploy a Drupal 7 website.

2. Easily add exciting and powerful features.

3. Design and implement your website's look and feel.

4. Promote, manage, and maintain your live website.

Please check **www.PacktPub.com** for information on our titles

www.ingramcontent.com/pod-product-compliance
Lightning Source LLC
LaVergne TN
LVHW081345050326
832903LV00024B/1325